Cambridge Elements ☰

Elements in Psychology and Culture
edited by
Kenneth D. Keith
University of San Diego

CULTURE-INCLUSIVE THEORIES

An Epistemological Strategy

Kwang-Kuo Hwang
Research Center for Cultural China

CAMBRIDGE
UNIVERSITY PRESS

CAMBRIDGE
UNIVERSITY PRESS

University Printing House, Cambridge CB2 8BS, United Kingdom

One Liberty Plaza, 20th Floor, New York, NY 10006, USA

477 Williamstown Road, Port Melbourne, VIC 3207, Australia

314–321, 3rd Floor, Plot 3, Splendor Forum, Jasola District Centre,
New Delhi – 110025, India

79 Anson Road, #06–04/06, Singapore 079906

Cambridge University Press is part of the University of Cambridge.

It furthers the University's mission by disseminating knowledge in the pursuit of
education, learning, and research at the highest international levels of excellence.

www.cambridge.org
Information on this title: www.cambridge.org/9781108718653
DOI: 10.1017/9781108759885

First published 2019

A catalogue record for this publication is available from the British Library.

ISBN 978-1-108-71865-3 Paperback
ISSN 2515-3986 (online)
ISSN 2515-3943 (print)

Culture-Inclusive Theories

An Epistemological Strategy

Elements in Psychology and Culture

DOI: 10.1017/9781108759885
First published online: August 2019

Kwang-Kuo Hwang
Research Center for Cultural China
Author for correspondence: Kwang-Kuo Hwang, kkhwang@ntu.edu.tw

Abstract: The author proposes an epistemological strategy to resolve controversial issues in the indigenous psychology (IP) movement. These include the nature of IPs, scientific standards, cultural concepts, philosophy of science, mainstream psychology, generalization of findings, and the isolation and independence of IPs. The approach includes a two-step strategy for construction of culture-inclusive theories, based on a Mandala model of self and a *Face and Favor* model for social interaction, and the use of these models to develop culture-inclusive theories for Confucian morphostasis. The author and his colleagues have successfully used this strategy, and encourage others to use it to construct their own culture-inclusive theories.

Keywords: culture-inclusive theories, critical realism, analytical dualism, scientific microworld, Confucianism

ISBNs: 9781108718653 (PB), 9781108759885 (OC)
ISSNs: 2515-3986 (online), 2515-3943 (print)

Contents

1 East Meets West   1

2 Relativism vs. Universalism   7

3 An Epistemological Strategy for Cultural Analysis   12

4 Universal Models of Self and Social Interaction   29

5 The Construction of Culture-Inclusive Theories   38

6 Conclusion   56

   References   58

1 East Meets West

In his discourse on the *general* background conditions for the development of the indigenous psychologies (IPs), Allwood (2018) cited Basalla's (1967) model of three stages for the historical spread of Western science to non-Western countries. In the first stage, non-Western countries simply provided resources for European or Western science. Data related to flora, fauna, geography, and anthropology were collected by Western explorers and their non-Western assistants. In the second stage of *colonial science*, non-Western researchers in a discipline are dependent on the research community in one or more Western countries for their development. In the third stage of *independent scientific tradition*, the non-Western nation establishes a full-fledged research community of its own, including its own institutions and Ph.D. education.

The emergence of the indigenization movement in psychology can generally be conceived as the second stage of Basalla's model. My major argument in this Element is that a comprehensive understanding of Western philosophy of science is necessary for non-Western countries to develop a full-fledged independent social science. If non-Western nations cannot provide an adequate program of education in philosophy of science for their Ph.D. students, their scientific community might be trapped in a dilemma of self-colonization.

In his section on "Specific Conditions for the Development of IPs," Allwood (2018) suggested classification of types of IPs into South and East Asian IPs with subtypes, Nationalistic IPs (e.g., the Philippines), IPs in the Muslim world (specifically in Iran), Oceanian (e.g., Australian and New Zealand) and fourth-world IPs, very small size IPs (e.g., African IPs in the Cameroon and Ghana), and Western IPs (e.g., Canadian). Such a post hoc classification seems plausible. But it seems to me that East Asian IPs in Taiwan, China, Korea, and Japan, with a similar cultural heritage of Confucianism, should be classified as an independent type. The reason can be explained from the perspective of anthropology of knowledge.

1.1 Archaeology of Knowledge in the West and China

Adair (2006) argued that the need for indigenization depends on the difference between the culture of the IP researcher and the US culture; therefore, the need for indigenization is "greatest in Asia and Africa, much less in Latin America, even less in Europe and probably least in Canada" (p. 470). This argument is acceptable. Nevertheless, he cautioned against spending too much attention on early religious or philosophical writings (Adair, 1996). Viewed from the archaeology of knowledge advocated by Foucault (1966), his warning is unsophisticated. On the contrary, the anthropology of knowledge in a given culture should be traced back to its historical origin.

1.1.1 Cultural Origin of Western Science

In his classical work *The Origin and Goal of History*, the eminent German philosopher Karl Jaspers (1953) indicated that the 600 years from 800 BC to 200 BC was the axial age for the progress of human civilizations. Groups of thinkers emerged simultaneously during this age in four separate and independent areas of the world. Their thoughts had been summarized by four paradigmatic figures, namely, Buddha (566–486 BC), Socrates (470–399 BC), Confucius (551–479 BC), and Jesus. Buddhism was imported into China during the first century of the Han dynasty to mix with Taoism and Confucianism that constituted the most significant future of Chinese civilization.

On the other side of the world, during the period from 1096 to 1270, the religious Crusades facilitated cultural exchange between the Eastern and Western branches of Christendom, which had been divided since the East–West Schism of 1054. The implementation of ancient Greek philosophy into the Western world of Christianity resulted in the European Renaissance movement after the fourteenth century. The start of the scientific revolution in the 1620s initiated the age of Enlightenment. This intellectual and philosophical movement that dominated the world of ideas in Europe undermined the authority of the monarchy and the Church and paved the way for the political revolutions of the eighteenth and nineteenth centuries. The emergence of the philosophy of science in the twentieth century can trace its intellectual heritage to the Enlightenment.

1.1.2 Totalistic Anti-traditionalism in China

Western science was introduced into China by Jesuit priests in the seventeenth century. Nevertheless, because traditional organic science originating from the cosmology of yin/yang is essentially incompatible with the newly emerged Western mechanic science (Needham, 1969, 1978), it is very hard for Chinese intellectuals to understand the meaning as well as the substantial content of the imported science with their educational background of Confucian classics.

The defeat of China by Great Britain in the First Opium War (1839–1842) signified the beginning of the Century of Humiliation. During the period of intervention and imperialism by Western powers and Japan between 1839 and 1949, China suffered major internal fragmentation, lost almost all of the wars it fought, and was often forced to give major concessions to the great powers in the subsequent treaties. Due to the political chaos caused by civil wars among war lords in the early years of the Republic of China, three major ideologies prevailed among Chinese intellectuals in the period of the May Fourth Movement, namely, social Darwinism, scientism, and anti-traditionalism (Kwok, 1965). They believed that only democracy and science could save China from the crisis of dissolution. Because traditional Chinese culture was essentially different from Western culture, and both were absolutely incommensurable, "Mr. Confucius" must be replaced by two foreign Bodhisattvas, "Mr. Science" and "Mr. Democracy." As a consequence, modernization implied an ideology of "totalistic anti-traditionalism" in China (Lin, 1979).

These were the cultural and historical causes of the Cultural Revolution in Communist China from 1966 to 1976. The emergence and progress of the indigenization movement in the social sciences of Taiwan implies that another similar but different story happened in this small island.

1.1.3 May Fourth Ideologies

When Nationalist China retreated to Taiwan, Ching Kai-Shek brought about 1.3 million people with him to this island, which had a population of 6 million. Most of them were descendants of earlier Chinese immigrants who migrated to Taiwan from coastal areas of China in the Qing Dynasty. Only about 40 to 60 thousand of them were aboriginal people. About half of the 1.3 million new immigrants were soldiers of the Nationalist army, while the other half were "cultural elites" escaped from various provinces of China. They were the "five categories of disgraced people" (黑五類), including landlords, rich farmers, rightists, counter-revolutionists, and bad elements, who fled their homeland to avoid the political movements of the class struggle initiated by the communists.

After the end of World War II, all Japanese teachers in the educational system of Taiwan were sent back to Japan. Their vacancies were soon occupied by those Chinese elites taking refuge with the Nationalist government in 1949. They also brought to Taiwan the ideologies of the May Fourth Movement. The one-party political system in the Cold War era further provided social support for those ideologies. When the communist regime initiated a series of political movements in mainland China, escalating to the Cultural Revolution, the Nationalist government in Taiwan pushed forward the Chinese Cultural Renaissance Movement as an antagonistic response. Such cross-strait politics prompted liberal intellectuals to consolidate their ideologies of the May Fourth period. They generally believed it necessary to fight against the cultural tradition of one-party domination in the political system for the sake of promoting modernization through science and democracy of the American style.

1.1.4 Cultural Foundation of Self-colonization

Western philosophy of science addresses issues of ontology, epistemology, and methodology, reflecting on a scientist's ontological presumption about the subject of study, and critically examining the epistemological knowledge constructed on one's ontological presumption through various methods of empirical research. Notwithstanding, liberal intellectuals in Taiwan had established an academic tradition that indulged students in issues of methodology without intensive reflection on ontology and epistemology. Consequently, most Taiwanese graduate students tend to conduct empirical research following Western theories or paradigms, without knowing how to construct their own theories, let alone challenging imported Western theories.

The approach of naïve positivism or naïve empiricism without deliberate elaboration in philosophy of science can be viewed as a modern version of scientism, which might be the cultural foundation of self-colonization.

Here it should be noted that traditional China had its own educational system of colleges (書院) where Confucian classics were taught to intellectuals in preparation of civil examinations. After abolition of the civil examination system in 1905, the traditional colleges were replaced by a Western-style educational system. The ideologies of May Fourth, originating from the New Cultural Movement before 1919, have created in Chinese intellectuals a mentality of stagnation in *scientism*, and, lacking sophistication in philosophy of science, may hinder escape from the trap of self-colonization.

1.2 Two Approaches of IP in Taiwan

Allwood (2018: p. 8) is correct in indicating that "some engaged researchers have, at least to some extent, put their hallmark on specific IPs." In his analysis of the development of IP in Taiwan, he mentioned Kuo-Shu Yang and Kwang-Kuo Hwang as two representative IP figures in this area. He noted that Yang was a pioneer of IP in Taiwan who entered on a mission to Sinicize psychology in 1976; but he did not know Yang's major academic interest before 1976. He said:

> The IP in Taiwan has also been characterized by debates on what type(s) of IP should be developed. Here the distinction made by Virgio Enriquez between exogenous indigenization and endogenous indigenization is useful. As noted above, exogenous indigenization means a type of indigenization process where foreign thinking (typically Western) is used as a basis for the development of the country's IP and by endogenous indigenization is meant indigenization from within, that is, where no foreign thinking is used in the indigenization process. Yang (quoted in Hwang, 2005: p. 232) wrote in 1993 "What we mean by indigenous psychology is restricted to endogenous psychology, and that is what we seek." In contrast, Hwang (e.g., 2005, 2015) has repeatedly argued

that IP in Taiwan and elsewhere should be based on a methodological and philosophical platform from the West, that is, an exogenous type of indigenization process. (Allwood, 2018: p. 14)

1.2.1 Sensitivity to Colonization

Allwood concluded, "The current state of the IP in Taiwan is somewhat unclear" (2018: p. 14). In order to understand the current state, as well as the future development of IP in Taiwan and China, it is necessary to know Yang's historical background, his ultimate concern, and his relationship with K. K. Hwang (author of this monograph). Kuo-Shu Yang (1932–2018) was born in a village of Shandong, mainland China. He escaped to Taiwan with his family in 1947 to avoid the civil war between Nationalists and Communists. Under the influence of the May Fourth ideologies, he had a passion for modernization of Chinese society. He was an activist who had participated in many programs of political, social, and educational reform in his youth, with significant contributions to the democratization of Taiwan. Meanwhile, he was engaged in research on *individual modernity* reflecting naïve empiricism (Hwang, 2003a, 2003b, 2003c; Yang, 2003). This may be why Yang "did not mention the influence of colonialism and imperialism when he described the introduction of Western psychology in non-Western countries" (Allwood, 2018: p. 7).

My life story is different from that of Yang. I am a native Taiwanese. The island of Taiwan was colonized by Japan for a period of fifty years from 1895 to 1945, the year when I was born. My life experience makes me very sensitive to issues related to colonization. Yang was my mentor when I studied for the master's degree in the graduate school of psychology, National Taiwan University. I completed a thesis titled *Studies on Individual Modernity and Social Orientation* under his supervision (Hwang & Yang, 1972).

1.2.2 Paradigm Shift in Psychology

In those days, when I was studying in Taiwan, psychology was defined as "behavioral" science. The most influential paradigm in psychology was behaviorism, and personality was conceived as a "black box." Culture had no position at all in its formation.

I obtained a scholarship from the East-West Center, which enabled me to work for the Ph.D. degree at the University of Hawaii from 1972 to 1976. During that period, I experienced a cultural shock that caused me to reflect on the meaning of research in psychology. We had a famous professor, Arthur W. Staats, at UH who published a book titled *Social Behaviorism* and tried to explain all social behaviors in terms of several principles of S-R psychology.

But the textbook for our class in social psychology had a subtitle emphasizing that it adopted a *cognitive approach* (Stotland & Canon, 1972). My academic advisor, Anthony Marsella, was interested in studying psychopathology in various culture, and an eminent professor of philosophy, L. Lauden (1978), advocated for the psychology of pragmatism on our campus. This experience of multiple approaches in psychology enabled me to become aware that a *paradigm shift* was occurring in the field, and that various paradigms in Western psychology have their own philosophical grounds.

1.2.3 Face and Favor Model

My experience studying abroad had a profound influence on my research orientation after I returned to Taiwan and began my academic career at the National Taiwan University in 1976. Kuo-Shu Yang initiated an indigenization movement in psychology during the early years of the 1980s (Yang & Wen, 1982). I soon realized that most Western theories of psychology had been constructed on the presumption of individualism, but that most non-Western cultures emphasize the importance of interpersonal relationships, which was relatively neglected by Western psychologists. Therefore, I constructed a *Face and Favor* model to describe the mechanism of dyad interaction between two parties of various relationships (Hwang, 1987). Then I used this model as a framework to analyze the content of Confucianism and published a book, *Confucianism and the East Asia Modernization* (Hwang, 1988).

1.2.4 Philosophy of Science

Because my approach was very different from the typical ways of doing psychological research, it was strongly questioned by others within the camp of indigenous psychology in Taiwan. The experience of debating with others reminded me of the relationships between Western psychology and philosophy of science which I had learned at UH. Because philosophy of science is a product of Western civilization, it is very hard for Chinese scholars to understand the dialectical relationships among various paradigms of philo-sophy. So I decided to write a book to help other Chinese scholars understand the meaning of my approach for promoting the progress of indigenous psychology.

I spent more than ten years writing the book *Logics of Social Science* (Hwang, 2001/2003/2018a), which addresses different perspectives on crucial issues of ontology, epistemology, and methodology proposed by eighteen Western philosophers since the beginning of the twentieth century. The first half of this book discussed the philosophical switch of nature science from positivism to post-positivism. The second half expounded the philosophy of social science, including structuralism, hermeneutics, and critical science.

1.2.5 Confucian Relationalism

The experience of writing this book fostered in me an attitude of postcolonialism, but not anti-colonialism, in my career of developing IP (Hwang, 2005). It is one of my eternal beliefs that in order to overcome the difficulties encountered in the work of theoretical construction, non-Western indigenous psychologists have to understand not only their own cultural tradition, but also the Western philosophy of science. Therefore, I disagree with Allwood's (2018: p. 14) argument that my approach means "an *exogenous* type of indigenization process." I don't think that the distinction between *exogenous* indigenization and *endogenous* indigenization has sound philosophical implications, nor can it make a significant contribution to the future progress of IP.

Based on such a belief, since the beginning of 2000 when I was appointed as principal investigator of the *Project in Search of Excellence for Research on Chinese Indigenous Psychology* by the Ministry of Education in Taiwan, I have constantly attempted to resolve the difficulties of constructing culture-inclusive theories in psychology by using various paradigms in the Western philosophy of science. When the project was finished in 2008, I integrated findings from previous related research into a book titled *Confucian Relationalism: Philosophical Reflection, Theoretical Construction and Empirical Research* (Hwang, 2009); its English version was published with a new title, *Foundations of Chinese Psychology: Confucian Social Relations* (Hwang, 2012).

2 Relativism vs. Universalism

The *Asian Association of Social Psychology* sponsored its third International Conference with the theme "Striving for a New Era for Asian Social Psychology" in Taipei, Taiwan, August 4–7, 1999. Kuo-Shu Yang, as the organizer of this conference, invited six distinguished scholars to give keynote speeches on the future development of IP from the perspectives of cross-cultural psychology, cultural psychology, and indigenous psychology. All these keynote speeches were published as a special issue of *Asian Journal of Social Psychology* (Hwang & Yang, 2000).

2.1 A New Emerging Field

Unlike cultural psychology and cross-cultural psychology, whose theoretical positions have long been established elsewhere and are well known to most in the field of social psychology, indigenous psychology is a relatively new and emerging field. Its conceptualization and theoretical directions remain unsettled and are still subject to more debates and reformulation. I was fortunate to meet three key people whose theoretical or philosophical stances are very helpful as I sought solutions to overcome difficulties encountered in developing IP in Confucian culture. They were Richard Shweder, Fritz Wallner, and Patricia Greenfield. Shweder gave me an important principle of cultural psychology: "One mind, many mentalities"; Wallner reminded me of the necessity of making a distinction between the scientific microworld and lifeworld; and Greenfield emphasized the importance of structuralism.

Their suggestions, along with my knowledge of the philosophy of science, enabled me to define the goal of IPs, to resolve the controversial debate about the relation between IPs and other types of psychology, and to formulate my epistemological strategy for constructing culture-inclusive theories in psychology. All these issues are closely related, and will be elaborated in the following sections of this monograph.

2.1.1 Bottom-up Model Building Paradigm

Generally speaking, indigenization movements have been initiated by non-Western psychologists in a spirit of nationalism and academic anticolonialism. They have argued that current mainstream psychology is basically a kind of Westernized or Americanized psychology. Both its theory and research methods contain Western ethnocentric bias (Berry et al., 1992). When the Western psychology research paradigm is transplanted blindly to non-Western countries, it is usually irrelevant, inappropriate, or incompatible for understanding the mentalities of non-Western people (Sinha 1984, 1986). Such a practice has been regarded as a kind of academic imperialism or colonialism (Ho, 1993). By ignoring the fact that many Western theories of social psychology are culturally bound, duplication of a Western paradigm in non-Western countries may result in neglect of cultural factors that may influence the development and manifestation of human behavior (Hwang, 2006).

As a reaction to the state of being colonized, many indigenous psychologists have advocated "a bottom-up model building paradigm" (Kim, 2000: p. 265) to promote "the study of human behavior and mental processes within a cultural context that relies on values, concepts, belief systems, methodologies, and other resources" (Ho, 1998: p. 71), and that treats people "as interactive and proactive agents of their own actions" that occur in a meaningful context (Kim, Park, & Park, 2000: p. 71). They perform a "scientific study of human behavior (or the mind) that is native, which is not transported from other regions and that is designed for its peoples" (Kim & Berry, 1993: p. 2) in order to develop a "cultural-appropriate psychology" (Azuma, 1984: p. 53), "a psychology based on and responsive to indigenous culture and indigenous realities" (Enriquez, 1993: p. 158), or a psychology whose "concepts, problems, hypotheses, methods, and tests emanate from, adequately represent, and reflect upon the cultural context in which the behavior is observed" (Adair, Puhan, & Vohra, 1993: p. 149).

2.1.2 Challenges to Indigenous Psychology

The legitimacy of *relativism* implied in this approach was challenged by cross-cultural psychologists who advocated for a symbiosis of cultural and comparative approaches. For example, Triandis (2000) pointed out that anthropologists have used a similar approach for years, and that accumulating anthropological data with an idiosyncratic approach may not have much significance in terms of contribution to the development of scientific psychology. Poortinga (1999) indicated that the usage of the plural "indigenous psychologies" by many indigenous psychologists suggests an implicit restriction on the potential for development of indigenous psychology. The development of multiple psychologies not only contradicts the scientific requirement of parsimony, but also makes the demarcation of cultural populations a pending problem. If every culture has to develop its own psychology, how many indigenous psychologies should there be? How many psychologies would have to be developed for Africa? What is the optimal number of indigenous psychologies? What is the meaning of an indigenous psychology developed in a specific culture to people in other cultures?

Ho (1988), a supporter of indigenous psychology, advocated the development of an Asian psychology, but also pointed out that if every culture develops its own psychology, another kind of ethnocentrism in reverse would arise. Poortinga (1996: p. 59) has similar criticisms, arguing that overemphasis on the nature and extent of differences in psychological functioning between people of different cultures may make indigenous psychology a kind of "scientific ethnocentrism in a new guise."

2.1.3 Final Goal of Indigenous Psychology

In order to seek common ground for cross-cultural comparison, cross-cultural psychologists advocated for the position of *universalism* instead of *relativism*. For instance, Poortinga (1999: p. 425) strongly suggested that "differences in behavioral repertoires across cultural populations should be understood against the background of a broader frame of commonness." He argued that overemphasis on cross-cultural differences in behaviors and negation of important commonalities in psychological functioning across different cultures is not only "factually incorrect," but also "theoretically misleading" (p. 419).

In order to respond to these challenges, most indigenous psychologists have argued that the development of numerous indigenous psychologies is not their final goal. Rather, their final goal is to develop an Asian psychology (Ho, 1988), a global psychology (Enriquez, 1993), a universal psychology (Kim & Berry, 1993), or a human psychology (Yang, 1993). To achieve this goal, they have proposed several research methods or approaches, including the derived etic approach (Berry, 1989), the metatheory method (Ho, 1998), and the cross-indigenous method (Enriquez, 1977), as well as cross-cultural indigenous psychology (Yang 1997). Yang (2012) argued that all those methods or approaches are designed to achieve the final goal of genuine, global human psychology.

Unfortunately, as Allwood (2018) indicated in his review, none of those final goals has been achieved by indigenous psychologists with any of these methods. In order to set an appropriate goal for IP to pursue, it is necessary for us to clarify the relationships among indigenous psychologies, cultural psychology, and cross-cultural psychology.

2.2 IP and Cultural Psychology

In their earlier works on IP, Kim and Berry (1993: pp. 21–22) claimed, "The closet sibling to the indigenous psychologies is cross-cultural psychology," because "the indigenous psychology approach represents indigenization from within, whereas the cross-cultural psychology approach represents indigenization from without." In fact, these two approaches are not mutually exclusive, but complement each other. Later, Ho (1998: p. 101) agreed that "indigenous psychologies are best regarded as a subdomain of cross-cultural psychology."

2.2.1 One Mind, Many Mentalities

Nevertheless, after the beginning of the 2000s, another group of IP authors criticized the abstract comparative approach of cross-cultural psychology (e.g., Hwang, 2015; Kim et al., 2000; Kim, Yang, & Hwang, 2006), and declared their affinity to the cultural psychology advocated by Michael Cole (1996) and Richard Shweder (1990), both of whom argued for the study of intentional activities carried out by people striving to attain goals in their everyday life. Furthermore, Shweder (1990) has strongly argued against the so-called Platonic central processing mechanism which assumes that people operate in a context-free environment. He concluded that there is little difference between cultural psychology and IP – they "are exactly on the same page" (Shweder, 2000: p. 221) – and proposed an important principle for both of them to follow: "one mind, many mentalities" (Shweder, 1996, 2000; Shweder et al., 1998).

This phrase indicates that the psychological functioning or mechanisms of the human mind are the same all over the world, but that people may evolve various mentalities in different social and cultural environments. The goal of achieving a global psychology entails the expectation that the knowledge system constructed by indigenous psychologists should reflect not only the universal human mind, but also the particular mentality in a given culture. Indigenous psychologists should incorporate both cultural variation and cross-cultural invariance into their research schemes. This goal cannot be achieved by the inductive approach as suggested by those indigenous psychologists who insist on the philosophy of positivism. Closer examination of the terms *mind* and *mentality* reveals the reason the inductive approach is insufficient.

2.2.2 Global Community Psychology

According to Shweder's (2000) definition, *mind* means "the totality of actual and potential conceptual contents of human cognitive process," and *mentality* denotes "the cognized and activated subset of mind" (p. 210). A mentality is owned or exercised by some group of particular individuals, so it can be a subject for research in cultural psychology. In contrast, mind refers to all the conceptual content that any human being might ever cognize and activate or represent. This universal mind cannot become the subject of research in cultural psychology. If indigenous psychologists want to achieve the goal of universalization with the inductive approach, they would have to carry out a very large-scale research program traveling around the globe to investigate all indigenous psychologies. Moreover, they would also have to take into account what has been manifested in the history and even the future of each culture (Wallner & Jandl, 2006). Obviously, this is a mission: impossible. So, how can indigenous psychologists solve this dilemma and achieve the goal of a global psychology?

Marsella (1998) advocated the development of a global community psychology, defined as a set of premises, methods, and practices for psychology based on multicultural, multidisciplinary, and multinational foundations that are global in interest, scope, relevance, and applicability. To achieve this goal, researchers from different regions around the world should be encouraged to explore their indigenous traditions and characteristics of different cultural groups. In their explorations, researchers worldwide should work on academic or research problems that are mutually relevant in diverse local contexts. The multiplicity of indigenous psychologies constructed by multiple paradigms may enrich the psychological discipline, facilitate the progress of a global community psychology (Marsella, 1998), and enable counseling professionals to enhance their global perspectives (Leong & Blustein, 2000) and multicultural awareness (Hwang, 2018a).

2.2.3 An Epistemological Strategy to Be Explained

Inspired by Marsella's idea of global community psychology, my epistemological strategy has been designed to resolve the dilemma between universalism and relativism faced by IP researchers (Hwang, 2018b). In the final part of his long section of discourse on "the Issues of Isolation and Independence," Allwood (2018) said,

> Hwang (e.g., 2005, 2015) exemplifies an IP author who has wholeheartedly argued that IP researchers should not limit themselves to influence only by thinking from their own culture. Hwang argued that it is necessary for IPs to use Western philosophies of science in order to promote and make progress in their research. For example, he (2015) wrote "It is one of my eternal beliefs that in order to overcome the difficulties encountered in the work of theoretical construction, non-Western IPists have to understand not only their own cultural tradition, but also the Western philosophy of science" (pp. 9–10). From this he argued that IP researchers should use the philosophical frameworks he prefers, namely those of the philosopher and sociologist Roy Bhaskar and his critical realism, and the philosopher Fritz Wallner and constructive realism. Doing this would make IP researchers able to compete with researchers in Western mainstream psychology. Similarly, de Souza (2014) suggested that the IPs should adopt a Western derived framework, namely critical realism. (pp. 54–55)

As a result of my long-term debate with him (Hwang, 2011c, 2013, 2015), Allwood obviously understands my epistemological strategy for constructing culture-inclusive theories to a certain extent. However, I wonder why he did not discuss my epistemological strategy in the section on views on the philosophy of science, before reaching the "Conclusion" section of his monograph, thus neither elaborating my epistemological strategy to make it clear enough for latecomers to understand, nor using it to resolve many controversial issues occurred in the field of IP. Therefore, in this Element, I will use my approach for studying Confucian ethics and morality as an example to illustrate my epistemological strategy for cultural analysis; then I will try to resolve several major controversial issues encountered by indigenous psychologists.

3 An Epistemological Strategy for Cultural Analysis

In my book *Dialects for the Subjectivity of Confucian Cultural System* (Hwang, 2017b), I compared five epistemological strategies seeking cultural subjectivity

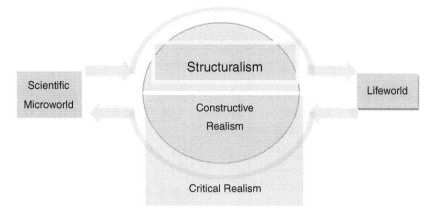

Figure 3.1 Epistemological strategy for constructing culture-inclusive theories

and emerging during the previous forty years of the indigenization movement of psychology in Taiwan. My epistemological strategy of cultural analysis appears in Figure 3.1. This figure shows that *constructive realism* (Wallner, 1994) and *critical realism* (Bhaskar, 1975, 1978) are the two major philosophies of science that constitute my epistemological strategy: *Constructive realism* insists on the separation between *scientific microworlds* and *lifeworlds; critical realism* provides a philosophy for constructing a *scientific microworld* that highlights the importance of *mechanism* for generating various phenomena in one's lifeworld, while structuralism can be used to link the generative *mechanism* of the scientific *microworld* and one's activities in the *lifeworld*.

3.1 Constructive Realism

Constructive realism is a philosophy of science proposed by the Vienna School after World War II in an attempt to synthesize numerous microworlds which were constructed by scholars in various fields of academic work (Wallner, 1994; Wallner & Jandl, 2006). As a result of rapid development in each field of science, different scholars may have constructed their own systems of knowledge regarding the same topic. How can they communicate with other with their own systems of knowledge?

In order to provide an answer to this question, the philosophy of constructive realism differentiated three levels of reality, the most important of which is called the *actuality* or *wirklichkeit*. The actuality is the world in which we find ourselves, or the given world that all living creatures must rely on to survive. The given world may have certain structures, or may function by its own rules. However, humans have no way to recognize these structures or rules. No matter how humans attempt to explain these structures, the explanation, and therefore our comprehension, is always a construction of human beings.

3.1.1 Lifeworld and Microworld

The world as constructed by human beings can be divided into two categories: lifeworld and microworld. Human beings construct these two worlds with different ways of thinking, which are supported by different types of rationalities. The knowledge created in each construction results in different worldviews with distinct functions. These two worlds constitute two levels of constructed reality for human beings.

The first constructed reality is the lifeworld in which humans live. For the individual, a lifeworld is a primordial world in which everything presents itself in a self-evident way. Before human beings began to develop scientific knowledge, they tried to understand their experiences in daily life, and to make various explanations, structures, and responses to their lifeworlds. These explanations and responses belonged to a domain of prelogical, pretechnical and pre-instrumental thinking, and their richness lies in individual life experiences (Husserl, 1970).

Lifeworlds are constantly sustained by a transcendental formal structure called cultural heritage. Language is the most important carrier of cultural heritage. People use language to play games as they interact in their lifeworlds. A *language game* is any kind of human practice or activity shared by people living in a given culture, which constitutes various forms of life. *Forms of life* refer to patterns of thinking that are manifest in cultural heritage, such as customs, folkways, institutions, and traditional practices in a particular historical and cultural condition. Language games are inevitably rooted in these forms of life (Wittgenstein, 1945/1958).

3.1.2 Scientific Microworld

Guided by various themes for different needs, human beings have constructed many kinds of microworld to explain or to understand various aspects of their lifeworlds, including religious, ethical, or aesthetic, but the most important one for us here is the scientific microworld. Because each thematic world is constructed with a particular way of thinking under the guidance of a certain theme, all phenomena irrelevant to that theme will be excluded. Therefore, each microworld bears a predetermined partiality and narrowness.

Any scientific construction can be regarded as a microworld. A scientific microworld can be a theoretical model built on the basis of realism, or a theoretical interpretation of a social phenomenon provided by a social scientist

Table 3.1 Two types of knowledge in lifeworld and scientific microworld

	Lifeworld	**Scientific microworld**
Constructor	Cultural group	Single scientist
Ways of thinking	Originative thinking	Technique thinking
Types of rationality	Substantive rationality	Formal rationality
Patterns of construction	Participative constructive	Dominative construction
Functions of worldview	Meaning of life	Recognition of world

from a particular perspective. Within any given scientific microworld, the reality of the given world is replaced by a second-order constructed reality that can be corroborated.

The construction of the scientific microworld is a product of Western civilization; many philosophers have tried to describe the significant features of knowledge in the scientific microworld, in contrast to that of lifeworlds, from different perspectives after the Enlightenment of the seventeenth century. Some of them appeared in my article "The Discontinuity Hypothesis of Modernity and Constructive Realism: The Philosophical Basis of Indigenous Psychology" (Hwang, 2000), and appear in Table 3.1.

3.1.3 Originative Thinking and Technical Thinking

People living in the same culture over a long period of evolution construct the natural language used in a lifeworld. In the formative years of a particular culture, people concentrate on observing and contemplating the nature of every object in their lifeworld. They rid themselves of their own will and intention, and try their best to make all things manifest in the language they create to represent it. Heidegger (1966) labeled this way of thinking *originative thinking*.

The language and way of thinking scientists use to construct theoretical microworlds are completely distinct from those used by people in their lifeworlds. Scientific knowledge is not obtained by contemplating the nature of things. Instead, scientists intentionally created it to reach a specific goal, so it has a compulsory and aggressive character that demands the most gain with the least cost. Such *technical thinking* has no interest in representing things in the objective world, and making things the object of knowledge. Instead, this type of thinking attempts to exploit natural resources by every means, and to transfer them into the storage of human beings.

Therefore, we may have many scientific microworlds, each of them constructed by a single scientist, while knowledge in a lifeworld has been contributed by numerous members of a cultural group.

3.1.4 Substantive Rationality and Formal Rationality

Technical thinking uses certain ground principles as a foundation. Modern people calculate their thinking with reference to a ground principle which serves as the foundation for rational thinking. But what is meant by *rationality*? Is the originative thinking needed by people in their lifeworlds irrational or lacking in rationality?

These questions can be answered through a consideration of Max Weber's works on comparative religion. In order to investigate the cause of the rise of industrial capitalism in the modern world, Weber (1921/1963; 1930/1992) proposed a set of contrasting concepts to highlight the unique features of Western civilization. He indicated that with the occurrence of the Renaissance in the fourteenth century, many western European countries experienced an expansion of rationalism in such fields as science, law, politics, and religion. He noted that the unique feature of *formal rationality* characterized the rationalism manifested in Europe after the Renaissance, which was completely different from the *substantive rationality* emphasized in other civilizations. Formal rationality emphasizes the calculability of means and procedures that can be used to pursue personal goals, and pays attention only to value-natural facts. In contrast, substantive rationality refers to the value of ends or results judged from a particular position, and provides no clear-cut means and procedures for reaching goals (Brubaker, 1984).

According to Weber's conceptual framework, all microworlds constructed by scientists contain the essence of formal rationality. Such microworlds of scientific knowledge are products of construction attained by scientists who are doing research in a specific domain utilizing the Cartesian way of thinking that emerged after the European Renaissance of the fourteenth century. It is essentially different from the way of constructing knowledge used by non-Western people in their lifeworlds.

3.1.5 Participative Construction and Dominative Construction

This point can be illustrated with Levy-Bruhl's (1910/1966) anthropological study of primitive thinking. His pioneering work in this field indicated that the cultural system of any primitive people, including their mythology and religion, is constituted on a basis of the law of mystical participation (Evans-Prichard, 1964), which conceptualizes human beings as parts of an inseparable entity that can be viewed as a consciousness of cosmic holism (Tylor, 1871).

In a premodern or primitive culture, the collective representation constituted by the law of mystical participation would seldom be refuted by empirical experience. Tradition and authority protect the culture from challenges by antagonistic information. Members of the community usually experience collective representations with shared sentiment, rather than examining them with empirical facts. People in many premodern cultures describe people and objects encountered in various situations with abundant vivid language. By doing so, they develop a rich lexicon in which the meanings of words are not only flexible, but can also be reshaped with the variation of experiences, people, and objects.

In premodern civilizations, people construct the knowledge in their lifeworlds through *participative construction* (Shen, 1994). The scientific microworlds constructed by Westerners with the philosophy of Cartesian dualism can be called *dominative construction*. Knowledge constructed in these two ways is completely different in nature and mutually incompatible.

3.1.6 Two Worldviews

The language games people play usually entail a particular worldview. The worldviews in the lifeworld and the microworld are essentially different. Walsh and Middleton (1984) indicated that the worldview in a given culture usually answers four broad categories of questions: Who am I? What is my situation in life? Why do I suffer? How do I find salvation? A worldview not only describes human nature but also the relationship between humans and the world, as well as one's historical situation in the world. It provides a diagnosis for problems and prescribes a recipe for their solution.

The worldview in a microworld does not have such a function. In his lexicon theory, Kuhn (1987) indicated that the scientific lexicon is composed of a set of terms with structure and content, which constitute an interrelated network. Scientists use terms in the lexicon to make propositions in a theory for describing the nature of the world. Scientific lexicons contain a particular way of seeing the world. Members of the same scientific community must master the same lexicon, understand meanings of each term, and share the same worldview in order to communicate with one another, think about the same problem and engage in related research in the same scientific community. But, the microworld worldview provides no answers to problems related to the meaning of life.

3.2 Critical Realism

The construction of a scientific microworld is mainly a product of Western civilization. It is not easy for a non-Western indigenous psychologist to have a comprehensive understanding of the progress of the Western philosophy of science. This might be one reason why indigenous psychologists have encountered so many of the issues mentioned in Allwood's review, particularly in his sections on "Views on Philosophy of Science" (4.4) and "Scientific Standards" (4.3).

In the "Retrospect" section of his article "On the Rise and Decline of 'Indigenous Psychology,'" Jahoda (2016) said:

> The problem for the advocates of IPs is that practically all of them, including those from majority non-western cultures, had been trained in western academic institutions in a tradition they now wanted to largely reject. It is not surprising that this led to ambivalence if not actual conflict. This comes out most clearly in the treatment of "science". The dilemma was that of wanting IPs to share the prestige of science, while at the same time displaying a reluctance to be shackled by the demands of rigour; it tended to result in more flexible re-definitions of "science". (p. 177)

The aforementioned paragraph shows Jahoda's Euro-centric prejudice toward advocates of the IPs (Hwang, 2016). When Jahoda said that, "all of them ... had been trained in Western academic institutions in a tradition they wanted to largely reject," he was very proud of his Western tradition. When he said that IP advocates are facing a dilemma of "wanting IP to share the prestige of science, while at the same time displaying a reluctance to be shackled by the demands of rigour," his argument implies that he understood the rigorous demands of science, which is a prestige that can only be shared by a small group of Western elites like himself. When he said, "it tended to result in more flexible re-definitions of 'science,'" he suggested that there is a rigorous definition of science which must be defended by Western psychologists and which cannot be changed by any advocate of the IPs.

3.2.1 Intentional Learning Process

Jahoda's obvious prejudice toward advocates of the IPs should be analyzed in accordance with the principle of cultural psychology, "one mind, many mentalities" (Shweder et al., 1998). Here "mind" means "the totality of actual and potential conceptual contents of human cognitive process," and "mentality" denotes "the cognized and activated subset of mind" (Shweder, 2000: p. 210).

In thinking of the distinction between scientific microworld and lifeworld, if we conceptualize a given philosophy of science as scientific microworld, it contains conceptual contents constructed by a particular philosopher. Once it has been cognized and activated as a microworld, it can be learned and acquired by anyone with universal human "mind," including the advocates of IPs, if and

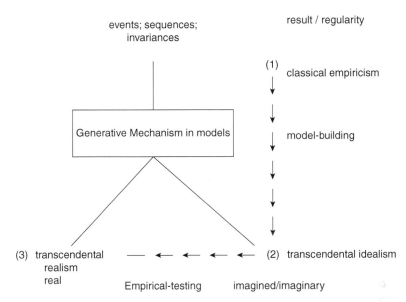

Figure 3.2 Philosophies for scientific discovery (adopted from Bhaskar, 1975: p. 174)

only if said advocate intends to learn and to acquire it. Without such a cognitive process of intentional learning, it is unlikely that anyone will understand either philosophy of science or "standards of science."

As I mentioned in the first section of this Element, my experience of learning in a Western academic institution (University of Hawaii) enabled me to realize that the crucial factor for promoting the indigenization of psychology lies in philosophy, not psychology itself. For the sake of helping Chinese IPists to overcome the major difficulties encountered in developing IP, I spent more than ten years studying the philosophy of science and published a book titled *The Logics of Social Sciences*, which systematically introduces the ontology, epistemology, and methodology proposed by seventeen major Western philosophers during the twentieth century. A new chapter on Bhaskar's (1975, 1978) work was added to the third edition of this book (Hwang, 2018a). A comprehensive understanding of Bhaskar's *critical realism* may save us from the danger of being dogmatic in talking about the "scientific standard," for it classified Western philosophies of science into three broad categories (Figure 3.2).

3.2.2 Empiricism

Classical empiricism was originally proposed by David Hume (1711–1776). It regards atomic facts as the ultimate objects of knowledge; their combinations constitute all the events which are objective to us in recognizing the external world. The logical structure of an elementary proposition stating relationships among names of objects is supposed to be isomorphic with that of the atomic fact in the objective world.

Positivism took a stance of radical empiricism. The method of induction was regarded as the main approach for acquiring knowledge through positivism; for instance, Wittgenstein (1889–1951), whose earlier works had profound influence on the Vienna Circle in the 1920s, maintained in his famous writing *Tractatus Logico- Philosophicus* that the main activity of science is to use language to describe the world. Atomic facts should be described with elementary propositions in a scientific theory that can be verified with empirical methods. Through the logical deduction of truth functions, elementary propositions can be combined into a scientific proposition. A proposition is a picture of reality, and the totality of true propositions reflects the nature of science as a whole (Wittgenstein, 1922).

3.2.3 Transcendental Idealism

The second category consists of transcendental idealism proposed by Kant and the various versions derived from it. According to this school, the goal of scientific activities is the construction of theoretical models to depict the natural order. Hence theoretical models are constructed by scientists, and though they might be independent from any particular individual, they cannot be independent from the scientific community.

According to this school, scientific research aims to find the underlying structure from its manifested phenomena. The constant association among events is the necessary but not sufficient condition for deriving natural law, and knowledge about the natural world becomes a construction of human minds. The modern version of this school argues that scientific knowledge is constructed by the whole science community.

3.2.4 Transcendental Realism

The third school of transcendental realism argues that scientific activities aim to find the mechanism for producing the phenomena. The objects of scientific research are neither the phenomena (empiricism) nor the constructs imposed on the phenomena (idealism), but the real structures which exist and operate independently from our knowledge. According to this perspective, the world exists independently from our knowledge about it. Both the world and our knowledge about it have their own structures which can be differentiated and are changing constantly. Science is not an epiphenomenon of nature, and nature is not a product manufactured by human beings.

3.3 Philosophical Switch from Positivism to Post-Positivism

The dramatic philosophical switch from the first category of empiricism to the second category of transcendental idealism may help us to understand the problematic situation faced by non-Western psychologists, while the third category of transcendental realism may provide some hints for solving those problems. Therefore, here I will first use Popper's philosophy to indicate the dramatic philosophical switch from the radical empiricism of positivism to the transcendental idealism of post-positivism (see Figure 3.2), then I will demonstrate how I utilize transcendental realism to explain my construction of culture-inclusive theories.

3.3.1 Ontology: Radical Empiricism or Realism

With active promotion by the Vienna Circle, logical positivism had an extraordinary influence on the thoughts of the scientific community from 1930–1950. When it reached the peak of academic prestige, it began receiving criticism from its academic opponents. The first challenge came from Karl Popper's evolutionary epistemology. Taking logical positivism and Popper's (1963, 1972) evolutionary epistemology as examples of positivism and post-positivism respectively, I compared the sharp contrast of their ontology, epistemology, methodology, as well as concept of person in Table 3.2.

In order to exclude all the metaphysics from the domain of science, logical positivism advocated radical empiricism for its ontology and argued that the only reality is what can be experienced by one's sensory organs. But Popper (1963) argued that scientific theories are not induced from empirical facts, but deduced by scientists with critical rationality. The procedure of scientific research should begin with a problem. When a scientist finds new empirical

Table 3.2 Ontology, epistemology, methodology, and concept of person in positivism and post-positivism

	Logical positivism	**Evolutionary epistemology**
Ontology	Radical empiricism	Realism
Epistemology	Truth	Approximation of truth
Methodology for discovery	Induction	Deduction with empiricism examination
Methodology for examination	Verification	Falsification
Concept of person	Solipsism	Agentic self

facts that cannot be explained, or inconsistencies in preexisting theories, a tentative solution or theory may be proposed to solve the problem. In order to explain the observed phenomenon or to answer an unsolved problem, the tentative theory may contain some metaphysical concepts that refer to noumena (or things in themselves) behind the phenomenon (Kant 1781/1965). The scientist must assume that the noumena are real; this position can be referred to as scientific realism.

3.3.2 Epistemology: Truth or Approximation to Truth

Logical positivism assumes the position of a template theory and advocates that the only legitimate way for a scientist to recognize objects in the world is through their representations in his mind. It is unnecessary for scientists to seek the ultimate cause that creates the objective world beyond sensory experience. Such radical empiricism advocates for an epistemological view, believing that scientific theories represent truth.

In contrast, evolutionary epistemology adopts the ontology of "realism," which assumes that there exists an ontological reality beyond our sensory experience. A scientist has to construct a theory to describe the objective world by conjecturing about the nature of its noumena. Popper (1963) suggested, "Our intellect does not draw its laws from nature, but tries with varying degrees of success to impose upon nature laws which it freely invents" (p. 191). Because theory is nothing more than the conjecture made by a scientist, its epistemology views scientific theory as an "approximation to the truth," but not truth in itself.

3.3.3 Methodology for Discovery

In accordance with logical positivism, an elementary proposition describes atomic fact that has been repeatedly experienced by human beings. Elementary proposition is induced from previous experiences; scientific law is established through repetitive occurrence of the same fact. Popper strongly opposed the idea that scientific theory can be achieved by an accumulation of true propositions describing empirical facts. According to one of Popper's analogies, the water bucket of scientific theory will not be spontaneously full so long as scientists work hard to fill it with accumulated empirical facts. Instead, a theory is like a searchlight. Scientists must continuously bring up problems and make conjectures, so as to cast the light of theory on the future (Popper, 1972: pp. 431–457). If a theory records only previous findings, and nothing can be deduced from it except preexisting facts, what is the use of a theory?

The deductive method Popper advocated is not the traditional deduction grounded in axiomatic premises. Popper argued that the premises of deduction for a tentative theory of scientific conjecture should be repeatedly subjected to empirical examination. This method is called "deduction with examination."

3.3.4 Methodology for Examination: Verification or Falsification

Logical positivists divide the academic labor into two parts: Philosophers are specialized to analyze the formal structure of logic, while scientists are obligated to verify the elementary proposition of a scientific theory by experimental methods replicable by any other scientist. Therefore, Schlick (1936) proposed a famous statement that was followed by most logical positivists: "The meaning of a proposition is the method for its *verification*" (p. 337; emphasis added).

Popper also opposed the principle of verification as advocated by positivists. According to Popper, a theoretical proposition cannot be verified; it can only be falsified by empirical facts contradicting the theory. A scientific theory is stated with general predications. However, empirical facts are individually experienced. No matter how many times a particular experience is repeated, it cannot verify a proposition of general prediction. For instance, no matter how many white swans have been observed, the proposition of the general prediction "swans are white" still cannot be verified, because our observations cannot include all swans. Therefore, scientists cannot "verify" theoretical propositions, but only falsify them, or reserve them temporarily before they are falsified.

3.3.5 Concept of Person: Solipsism or Agentic Self

Logical positivism adopts a position of radical empiricism and argues that the only reality is the facts experienced by sensory organs (see Figure 3.3). However, how can a scientist match the representation in mind with the structure of the external world? The logical positivist argues that it should be validated by a third party using an objective method. This constitutes the most controversial issue of logical positivism: Who is the "third party" to make the judgment when a scientist cannot do so?

In order to answer this question, a logical positivist needs to construct an absolutely objective *transcendental self*. More specifically, the self of solipsism as advocated by logic positivists is a *philosophical self* or *metaphysical subject*; it is neither the *psychological self* nor the *subject* who can represent and think. In the process of scientific activity, the subjectivity of a researcher becomes "a point that cannot be extended outward and can even eventually disappear."

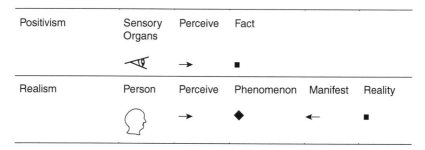

Figure 3.3 Epistemological tasks for positivist and realist

The concept of person in evolutionary epistemology is opposite to that of logical positivism. Viewed from the progress of Western philosophy, the solipsism implied in positivism is the most unique concept of person and reflects the Cartesian philosophy of dichotomy between subject and object. It assumes that the human being is a subject confronting the world. Scientists' major task is to describe the world objectively. Popper's evolutionary epistemology strongly opposes this position and advocates that science is a product of the creative activity of humankind. A scientist cannot passively await the accumulation of experience, but must be actively engaged in the tasks of criticism, creation, and validation (see Figure 3.3). These two philosophies harbor different concepts of person, and they thus hold opposing views of the role that a scientist should play in scientific activity. Most philosophers of science after Popper held similar positions about the agentic role of scientists in the process of theoretical construction, even though they may have various perspectives on what kind of knowledge scientists should pursue and how to pursue that knowledge.

3.4 Philosophy of Validation or Heuristics

Logical positivism was the philosophical ground for the psychology of *behaviorism*, while the construction of theories in *cognitive psychology* implies a philosophy of post-positivism. Most theories of cognitive psychology were constructed on the presumption of individualism by Western psychologists. When they are transplanted into non-Western countries and found to be inappropriate, or inadequate for explaining local phenomena, it is very hard for non-Western psychologists to construct their own culture-inclusive theories to compete with Western ones if they have been trained with the methodology of doing empirical research only. Without systematic training in ontology and epistemology of post-positivism for constructing culture-inclusive theories, they know only the philosophy of *validation* but not that of *heuristics*

(Lauden, 1977). This is the fundamental problem encountered by most non-Western advocates of IP.

3.4.1 Straw Man of Positivism?

Allwood (2018) was obviously lacking such an empathetic understanding when he said:

> Kim, Park, and Park (1999) used a concept they called "traditional psychology" to mean Western psychology up to about the 1970s, but which more obviously represents behaviorism in the first part of the twentieth century. Thus, their concept of "traditional psychology" is unclear, and is then used as a straw man to create a contrast to their Korean IP. Kim and Park (2005) also wrote that "General psychology has adopted positivism in search of abstract and universal laws of human behavior and eliminated the subjective aspects of human functioning (i.e. agency, meaning, intention and goals) and the influence of context and culture" (p. 75). It is not likely that many researchers involved in research in mainstream psychology in the 21st century would recognize this description as accurate! (p. 49)

Allwood's argument seems strange to me because it assumes that "many researchers involved in research in mainstream psychology in the 21st century" have a standard of "science" for making such a judgment in their minds. This is obviously an incorrect assumption for sustaining the hegemony of mainstream psychology. According to my experience developing IP in Confucian society, positivism of "traditional psychology" or behaviorism is definitely not "a straw man to create a contrast to" any Asian IP; it is a real and problematic situation for all Asian psychologists to deal with. Because most of them are lacking a comprehensive understanding of the progress of philosophy of science, they are consciously or unconsciously influenced by either positivism or logical positivism.

3.4.2 Accumulation of Empirical Findings

Allwood (2018) mentioned my criticisms of a number of methodological approaches to compare findings of empirical researchers from different societies suggested by IP researchers. He is correct in saying:

> The reason for his [Hwang's] criticism was that such approaches assume an inductive approach, in contrast to Popper's anti-inductive, deductive falsification approach. These approaches included Enriquez's cross-indigenous method (to compare results from IPs working with emic from-within approaches in order to look for higher-order generalizations) and the derived etic approach (to compare the results from etic and emic approaches) suggested by Berry and Kim (1993). (p. 50)

The limitation of an inductive approach by either an *imposed etic, expedient emic*, or *derived etic* approach with a mentality of positivism can clearly be seen by reviewing psychological research findings in a single culture for a long period of time. For instance, Michael Bond (2010) published the *Oxford Handbook of Chinese Psychology,* containing forty-one chapters by eighty-seven authors who intensively reviewed previous works on a variety of topics related to Chinese psychology. Nonetheless, with his careful review on this book, Lee (2011) indicated that he

> was somewhat puzzled and bothered by the fact that the book does not have a clear structure . . . It is thus difficult for readers to learn quickly about what is included in the book and to identify the chapter on a specific topic unless they go through the whole table of contents carefully. . . . The topic-oriented chapters have done a great job in reviewing and reporting extensively empirical findings in the field regarding the Chinese people. However, very few chapters offer indigenous theories of Chinese psychology (e.g. the chapter of Hwang and Han). Most of them stay at the level of confirming/disconfirming Western findings, referring to well-know cultural dimensions such as collectivism and power distance to explain the variation found, despite the openly stated effort to push for indigenous research. Moreover, most of the studies cited in the book simply dichotomized their findings as Chinese vs. Western, failing to capture the much more refined complexity of the world. (pp. 271–272)

The reason why most Chinese psychologists are indulged in "confirming/disconfirming Western findings, referring to well-known cultural dimensions such as collectivism and power distance to explain the variation found" is that most of them are well trained in methodology of validation only. The reason why "most of the studies cited in the book simply dichotomized their findings as Chinese vs. Western, failing to capture the much more refined complexity of the world" is that they know little about ontology and epistemology of heuristics in Western philosophy of science.

3.4.3 Limitation of Falsificationism

How to help Chinese psychologists to escape from the trap of indulgence in this type of empirical research? Allwood identified neither the fundamental problematic situation of non-Western IP, nor solutions to encounter the situation. He is correct in saying that I expressed an admiration for Karl Popper's philosophy of evolutionary epistemology in my long debate with him (Allwood, e.g. 2013). But he argued that

> arguments showing the limitations of Popper's falsificationism have been available for a long time in the philosophy of science literature, and it is not

clear that falsificationism is very much safer than inductionism. In a brilliant paper, Earp and Trafimow (2015) showed convincingly why Popper's falsification is not a more reasonable or stable path to follow in research than verification (or, as expressed by Hwang, inductionism). For example, results that appear to falsify a theory might as well be due to the falsifying study being a poor study in any of a number of ways. (p. 50)

Allwood is correct in indicating the limitations of Popper's falsificationism. He is also correct in arguing that falsificationism is not much safer than induction. In fact, this is a common ground for most philosophers of post-positivism after Popper (second category in Figure 3.2).

When logical positivism was criticized, Hempel, who had participated in the academic discussions of the Vienna Circle in earlier years, tried to modify its shortcomings and proposed the new idea of *logical empiricism*. In his *Aspects of Scientific Explanation*, Hempel (1965) proposed a *model of covering law*, which states that scientific explanation usually contains two kinds of statements, namely, general laws, and antecedent conditions. Using these two kinds of *explanans* as the premises, a scientist can deduct a description of a phenomenon, which is called the *explanandum*.

3.4.4 Creative Imagination

Hempel pointed out the difficulty of falsifying a hypothetical proposition. When scientists test a hypothesis, they must propose several auxiliary hypotheses that prescribe the antecedent conditions for its occurrence. Some of these auxiliary hypotheses are related to the scientific theory itself, and some to experimental design, instrumental equipment, or research procedures. A combination of all these conditions may lead to the occurrence of the phenomenon observed.

When scientists obtain a negative result from research, they rarely give up their general laws easily. Instead, they carefully examine their research instruments, reconsider the experimental design, or even repeat the experiment. These steps imply only consideration of whether there is anything wrong with the auxiliary hypotheses, indicating that it is not easy to falsify a hypothesis.

For this reason, Hempel (1965) argued that the target to be examined in scientific activity is not a sole hypothesis, but the whole theoretical system. Moreover, Hempel (1966) also believed that theory is not obtained by induction. It was impossible for a scientist to induce theory from empirical facts. For example, Newton's law of gravity and Einstein's theory of relativity were not inducted from a collection of observed phenomena. Scientists created them through imagination to explain what was observed.

The transition from data to theory requires creative imagination. Scientific hypothesis and theories are not derived from observed facts, but invented in order to account for them. They constitute guesses at the connections that might obtain the phenomena under study, at uniformities and patterns that might underlie the occurrence. (Hempel, 1966: p. 15)

3.4.5 Sophisticated Falsificationism

Lakatos (1971), one of Popper's students, also denounced Popper's falsificationism as a "naïve falsificationism" or "dogmatic falsificationism," claiming scientists will not easily give up propositions of a scientific theory once they are falsified by empirical research as Popper predicted.

Empirical refutation cannot easily eliminate errors in theory because propositions in scientific theory usually contain conditional sentences, *ceteris partibus*. Examination of a theoretical proposition should be carried out under specific conditions, no matter whether an experiment or observation is used. When an empirical fact obtained from an experiment or observation contradicts the prediction of the theory, a researcher is unable to ascertain whether the contradiction was caused by theoretical mistakes or by experimental or observational features. The famous Duhem-Quine thesis indicated that a theory can never be refuted if it is protected with auxiliary hypotheses. In other words, as long as a scientist is able to use imagination, auxiliary hypotheses may be proposed to attribute anomalies to other factors and to protect the core of the theory against falsification.

In Lakatos's (1970) view, the weakness of Popper's philosophy lies in the fact that it is unable to provide a sound basis for falsification. A scientific theory exists not in isolation, but as part of a series of theories with tight inner connections. Thus, Lakatos proposed a *sophisticated falsificationism* and advocated replacing the idea of theory with a series of theories, called a *scientific research program*. He suggested that the basic unit for examination in scientific research is neither a particular scientific proposition, nor an isolated theory, but rather a series of theories or a research program.

In summary, the sharp contrast between logical positivism and evolutionary epistemology as shown in Table 3.2 indicates that the two paradigms of positivism and post-positivism are incommensurable in every aspect of ontology, epistemology, and methodology, as well as role of person in scientific activities. Allwood's (2018) aforementioned discourse concentrated on the methodology of validation (i.e., verification/falsification of a scientific proposition by empirical research) only, but he ignored the ontology and epistemology of the heuristic for theoretical construction (Lauden, 1977), which is obviously too rough to catch the complicated problematic situation faced by advocates of IPs.

4 Universal Models of Self and Social Interaction

Allwood's (2018) discussion of the distinction between natural sciences and human sciences (i.e., the N/H distinction) was also oversimplified:

> Sundararajan et al. (2017) upheld the N/H-distinction by means of a controversial understanding of psychology when they argued that "General psychology represents the natural sciences approach, and indigenous psychology represents the cultural science tradition" (p. 1). However, many – maybe most – researchers in psychology may not agree that general psychology represents the natural sciences approach, partly because the N/H-distinction, as it is conventionally used, appears too coarse and as outdated. (p. 49)

It is easy to criticize the N/H-distinction as too coarse and outdated, but it is not easy to find a plausible way to integrate these two sciences. Allwood blamed advocates of IP without paying much attention to their endeavors for resolving the controversial issues. For instance, he noted the position of critical realism in my epistemological strategy of cultural analysis in his long-term debate with me (Allwood, 2018: p. 55), because deSouza (2014) also made similar suggestions. But the potential of Bhaskar's philosophy for dealing with issues of N/H-distinction was not seriously discussed.

4.1 Transcendental Idealism

Roy Bhaskar was brought up in London by his Indian father and British mother. He decided to study philosophy, politics, and economy when he attended Balliol College, Oxford University. When preparing his Ph.D. dissertation, he found that the economic development of developing countries can hardly be explained by Western theories of economy, so he transferred to the field of philosophy with a special interest in integrating natural and social science.

His philosophy was called "Transcendental Realism" in his earlier work, *A Realist Theory of Science* (Bhaskar, 1975), and changed to "Critical Naturalism" in his *Possibility of Naturalism* (Bhaskar, 1978). Because he insisted on a position of anti-positivism, rejected the challenges from postmodernism, and advocated for a rational science as well as the liberation function of philosophy, he was prompted to call his philosophy critical realism.

Bhaskar's (1975) epistemology was named transcendental realism. The term transcendental was used to denote the fact that his philosophy is supported by the so-called transcendental argument, which means the inference from an observed phenomenon to a lasting structure, or the inference from a particular real event to a more basic or more fundamental mechanism that makes the event possible. In Bhaskar's (1975: pp. 30–36) philosophy, the transcendental argument is a kind of retroductive argument which requires a scientist to retroduce the "structure on the condition for originating a phenomenon" from a "description of that phenomenon."

As I mentioned in the third section of this Element, Bhaskar proposed a figure to illustrate the three categories of scientific discovery.

4.1.1 Generative Mechanisms

Empiricism tries to find regularity from invariance of events in their sequences, but transcendental realism dialectically argues that regularity is the operational consequence of the same mechanism. Both transcendental idealism and transcendental realism emphasize model building, but the latter has to imagine how generative mechanisms produce the phenomena for scientific research. The mechanisms can be imaginary for transcendental idealism, but they need to be real for transcendental realism.

The epistemological strategy of my approach to study a cultural system was formulated in accordance with a fundamental principle of cultural psychology, namely, one mind, many mentalities; universalism without uniformity (Shweder et al., 1998: 871). This principle indicates that the psychological functioning or mechanisms of the human mind are the same all over the world, but that people may evolve diverse mentalities in different social and cultural environments. For the sake of achieving the goal of universal psychology, indigenous psychologists have to construct culture-inclusive theories to reflect not only the deep structure of universal human mind but also the mentalities of people in a particular culture.

Based on such a principle, my epistemological strategy for developing indigenous psychology consists of two steps: First, constructing universal models of *self* and *social* interaction; second, constructing culture-inclusive theories by using those models as frameworks for analyzing a given cultural tradition (Hwang, 2017a).

4.2 Face and Favor Model

Because all human beings are relational beings (Gergen, 2009), nobody can survive without social interaction. I had tried to construct a universal model of social interaction long before my attempt to construct a universal model of self. In chapter 4 of my book *Foundations of Chinese Psychology: Confucian Social Relations* (Hwang, 2012), I explained how I constructed the model of *Face and Favor* for depicting the universal mechanism of social interaction. In my theoretical model of *Face and Favor* (Hwang, 1987), the dyad involved in social interaction was defined as "petitioner" and "resource allocator." When the resource allocator is asked to allocate a social resource to benefit the petitioner, the resource allocator would first consider: "What is the *guanxi* (relationship) between us?"

4.2.1 Guanxi *and Rules for Exchange*

In Figure 4.1, within the box denoting the psychological processes of the resource allocator, the shaded rectangle represents various personal ties. It is first divided into two parts by a diagonal. The shaded part stands for the affective component of interpersonal relationships, while the unshaded part represents the instrumental component.

The same rectangle denoting *guanxi* (interpersonal relationships) is divided into three parts (expressive ties, mixed ties, and instrumental ties) by a solid line and a dotted line. These parts are proportional to the expressive component. The solid line separating expressive ties within the family and mixed ties outside the family indicates a relatively impenetrable psychological boundary between family members and people outside the family. Different forms of distributive justice or exchange rules are applicable to these two types of relationships during social interactions. In expressive ties, the need rule for social exchange should be adhered to and people should try their best to satisfy the other parties with all available resources. In mixed ties, following the *renqing* rule, when individuals want to acquire a particular resource from someone with whom they have instrumental ties, they tend to follow the equity rule and use instrumental rationality.

In my (1987) article, "Face and Favor: The Chinese Power Game," I elaborated the meaning of the *renqing* rule in Chinese society intensively. It is conceptualized as a special case of the *equality* rule, which emphasizes that once an individual has received favor from another, the individual is obligated to reciprocate in the future. Thus, the *Face and Favor* model can be viewed as a universal model applicable to different cultures. Is there evidence to support this argument?

4.2.2 Structuralism: Elementary Forms of Social Behavior

Following an intensive literature review of sociology, anthropology, and psychology research, Fiske (1991) proposed four elementary forms of social behavior in his book, *Structures of Social Life*. The four relational models are:

1. Communal Sharing: This is a relationship of equivalence in which people merge together to achieve the superordinate goals at hand so that boundaries among individual selves are indistinct. Group insiders have feelings of solidarity, unity, and belonging. They strongly identify with the collective

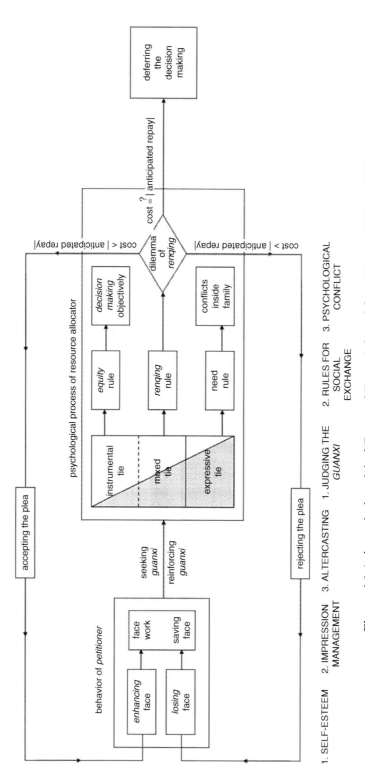

Figure 4.1 A theoretical model of *Face and Favor* (adopted from Hwang, 1987: p. 948)

and in some significant aspects think of themselves as an identical "we," instead of as an individual "I."

2. Authority Ranking: Individuals in this unequal relationship perceive each other as different in social importance or status. They can be ordered in a linear ranking, which may not translate across other ranking systems. Their ranking is hierarchical, with the high-ranking people controlling more persons, things, and resources. High-ranking individuals are also regarded as possessing more knowledge and mastery over events. The attention paid to them is asymmetric, with authority figures more salient than subordinates. Inferiors tend to show obedience and loyalty to their superiors, whereas leaders are entitled to provide protection and support to their followers.

3. Equality Matching: This is an egalitarian relationship among distinct and individual peers, each of whom has equal social presence including shares, contributions, and influence. Such one-to-one equality matching may manifest in turn-taking or in-kind reciprocity, where people exchange resources of the same value. These relationships entail matched contributions of the same kind and quantity. As a distributive justice, it takes the form of even distribution into equal parts among all people who prove indifferent about their portions. In the case of conflict or assignation, this relationship requires eye-for-an-eye retaliatory vengeance: if a person takes something, they have to compensate in equal measure, so that the exchange is balanced.

4. Market Pricing: This exchange relationship is mediated by the price determined in a market system. People evaluate others' actions, services, and products according to the rates at which they can be exchanged for other commodities. Money is the most important medium in market pricing, and people can decide whether to trade with each other based on this universal metric. Prior to making purchasing decisions, they can consider potential substitutes or complements, assess the temporal conditions of the market, and bargain with others out of self-interest.

4.2.3 Deep Structure of a Universal Mind

In *Structures of Social Life*, Fiske (1991) examined the manifestations and characteristics of these four elementary forms of human relations in various domains, including the aforementioned reciprocal exchange, distributive justice, and contribution, as well as work, meaning of things, orientations to land, social influence, constitution of groups, social identity and relational self, motivation, moral judgment and ideology, moral interpretation of misfortune, and aggression and conflict. He indicated that the four relational models are methods for human beings to organize their social domains. Manifestations of these four elementary forms of relations can be found in various situations, works, activities, domains of action, substantial problems, and attitudes, which implies that such structures are produced from the same psychological schemata or the deep structure of the universal mind.

Sundararajan (2015) compared Fiske's (1991) four elementary forms of relational models with my *Face and Favor* model (Hwang, 1987). Her results show that the three relational models of communal sharing, equality matching, and market pricing correspond with the expressive tie, the mixed tie, and the instrumental tie, as well as the three rules of exchange for the dyad of those relationships in the *Face and Favor* model, namely, the need rule, the *renqing* rule, and the equity rule. Moreover, the relationship between the petitioner and the resource allocator implies the power distance (Hofstede, 2001) or the authority ranking (Fiske, 1991) in the dyad of interaction. Such a comparison shows that Fiske's (1991) model provides a system for classifying elementary forms of social relations in human society, while my *Face and Favor* model was constructed as a universal mechanism of social interaction for human beings. From the perspective of constructive realism (Wallner, 1994), the core concepts in these two models can be translated from one model to the other. Therefore, the *Face and Favor* model was constructed to reflect the deep structure of the universal mind for interpersonal interactions.

4.3 Mandala Model of Self

I had a strong feeling that we were urgently in need of a new model of self when I was preparing my book on *Foundation of Chinese Psychology: Confucian Social Relations* (Hwang, 2012). The construction of my *Mandala model of self* was inspired by the insight that the structure of Borobudur Temple is a three-dimensional Mandala, which I noticed when visiting this site after the inaugural conference of the *Asian Association of Indigenous and Cultural Psychology* in July 2010 (Hwang, 2011a).

Borobudur Temple is located 40 kilometers northwest of Yogyakarta. The temple was built in the Sailendra dynasty, the rule of Java in the nineth century AD, and was the world's largest Buddhist building at the time. Then the temple sank because of volcanic eruption and lay hidden under dense jungle for almost one thousand years until the early nineteenth century. Now Borobudur, together with the Great Wall, the Pyramids and Angkor Wat, are known as the four wonders of the ancient Orient.

4.3.1 Mandala

I will begin my discussion of the Mandala model of self by introducing the meaning of Mandala. Mandala, a term from Tibetan Buddhism, is usually plotted in color as a symbol of the Buddhist cosmos, representing compassion and wisdom. Its basic structure is a circle inside a square. Lamas may spend one or two weeks using colored sand to build the Mandala during the festival of Tibetan Buddhism. There are strict rules for making a sand Mandala; the production process itself is a training in meditation and wisdom. The finished Mandala is colorful, symmetrical, magnificent, and solemn, bringing blessings to the festival and all of the participants.

At the end of the festival, lamas destroy the Mandala with their fingers. Colored sands are put into small bottles and distributed to the participants to take home for worship. The remaining sand is sprinkled on river or land. Accordingly, the Mandala also symbolizes the transformation of a Buddhist's life. The process from making a Mandala to its destruction represents the forming, staying, and emptying of one's existence.

The attitude involved in making and handling a Mandala contains the highest wisdom of Buddhism: Do everything seriously without taking it seriously. Buddhists believe in karma, the principal cause. People have to bear their own success and failure, so it is important to do everything seriously. However, Buddhists also believe in subsidiary causation: because things change in themselves, it is unnecessary to take them seriously.

4.3.2 Ultimate Goal of Life

The wisdom contained in the process of building a Mandala includes almost all the major ideas of self-cultivation in Oriental culture. The structure of a Mandala with a circle inside a square is a symbol of the self, representing the spiritual integrity to coordinate the relationship between human beings and the external world. In her article "Symbolism in the Visual Arts," published in a book titled *Man and His Symbols* edited by Jung (1964), Aniela Jaffe indicated that alchemists played an important role around 1000 AD, when various sects appeared in Europe. They sought for the integrity of mind and body and created many names and symbols.

Jaffe (1964) indicated that no matter where it is – in the sun worship of primitive people, in myths or dreams, in the Mandala plotted by Tibetan lamas, in modern religion, or in the planar graph of secular and sacred architectures in every civilization – the symbol of the circle represents the most important aspect of life, namely ultimate wholeness, whereas the square indicates secularity, flesh, and reality. Both symbols represent the most important aspects of one's life, and Mandala itself can be viewed as a symbol for the prototype, or the deep structure of one's self.

4.3.3 Person, Self, and Individual

In my Mandala model, *self* in the circle is situated in the center of two bi-directional arrows: One end of the horizontal arrow points at *action* or *praxis*, the other end points at *wisdom* or *knowledge* (see Figure 4.2). The top of the vertical arrow points at *person* and the bottom points at *individual*. All of these five concepts are located outside the circle but within the square. The arrangement of these five concepts indicates one's self is influenced by several forces from one's lifeworld. All the five concepts have special implications in cultural psychology, which needs to be elaborated in detail.

The distinction between person, self, and individual was proposed by Grace G. Harris (1989). Based on an intensive review of previous anthropological literature, she indicated that the triple structure of personality can be found in most cultures worldwide, but these three concepts have very different meanings in the Western academic tradition. As a biological concept, the individual regards each human being as member of the human species who is motivated to pursue some resources to satisfy their biological needs, which might be no different from other creatures in the universe.

Person is a sociological or cultural concept. A person is conceptualized as an agent-in-society who takes a certain standpoint in the social order and plans a series of actions to achieve a particular goal. Every culture has its own definitions of appropriate and permitted behaviors, which are endowed with specific meanings and values that can be passed on to an individual through various channels of socialization.

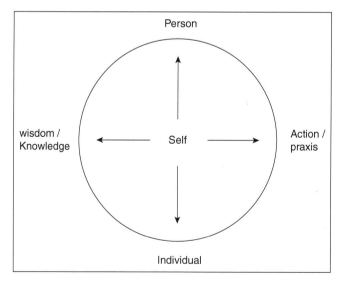

Figure 4.2 Mandala model of self (adopted from Hwang, 2011a: p. 330)

Self is a psychological concept. In the conceptual framework of Figure 4.2, self is the locus of experience that is able to perform various actions in different social contexts, while also able to indulge in self-reflection when blocked from goal attainment.

4.3.4 Habitus and Reflexivity

According to Giddens's (1984, 1993) structuration theory, the self as agency is endowed with two important capabilities, namely, reflexivity and knowledgeability. Knowledgeability means that the self is able to memorize, store, and organize various forms of knowledge, and transform them into a well-integrated system of knowledge. Reflexivity means that the self should have the wisdom to monitor his or her own actions, and is able to give reasons for such actions.

However, it is unnecessary for an individual to reflect on each of his or her actions. Giddens (1993) argued that one's practical consciousness enables one to be familiar with and even embody particular practical skills or knowledge in a tacit way. Bourdieu's (1990) constructivist structuralism used the term "habitus" to denote this kind of embodied and structuralized behavioral tendency. Habitus means an actor's disposition toward praxis or action in a specific social context that enables the actor to carry out the dynamic physical and mental practice within specific socio-cultural orders.

4.3.5 Personal Wisdom and Crystallized Intelligence

Baltes and his research team devoted many years to studying the wisdom of human beings at the Max Planck Institute in Berlin, Germany. They defined wisdom as a perfect state of Utopia, which is a collective product of culture, and argued that both culture and individual are carriers of wisdom (Baltes & Kunzmann, 2004). A distinction should be made between an individual's actual performance of wisdom and abstract existential wisdom of culture. In any cultural group of the world, there are some "wise men" whose realization of wisdom in life is frequently mentioned, discussed, or even imitated. Furthermore, there are many crystallized intelligences in any cultural heritage which may help its members to deal with major problems related to life planning, life management, and life review (Baltes, Dittmann-Kohli, & Dixon, 1984; Baltes & Smith, 1990).

Performance of acts and ideas of wisdom in one's daily life are actually manifestations of abstract cultural ideas. Therefore, one has to learn *wisdom-related knowledge* and store it in one's personal stock of knowledge which should be differentiated from the abstract culture ideas of existential wisdom stored in the social stock of knowledge.

An individual may bring his or her wisdom-related knowledge into full play when facing challenges in dealing with various core life issues and particularly when handling complicated affectional, interpersonal, or existential dilemmas. For example, Clayton (1982) and Kramer (1990, 2000) indicated that adult wisdom generally shows forth in five major domains: problem-solving, both establishing and leading an organization, life review, and spiritual self-cultivation. Sternberg (2000) also recognized that wisdom may be instrumental in coordinating one's personal interests with these of others and collectives.

5 The Construction of Culture-Inclusive Theories

In his book *Un sage est sans idèe: ou l'autre de la philosophie,* French philosopher François Jullien (1998) indicated that Chinese traditional thought – including Daoism, Confucianism, and Buddhism – is fundamentally different from that of Western philosophy. The teaching of Confucian, Daoist, and Buddhist sages should be called *wisdom* instead of *philosophy.* Western philosophy is deduced using dialectical reasoning based on certain *a priori* concepts. The term "concept" originates from the ancient Greek word *axiom* which Heidegger named the *principle of ground.* It is used as the first principle for deduction. On the contrary, Chinese traditional wisdom emphasizes "no speculation, no absolute definitude, no inflexibility, no selfishness." There are no prior concepts, no fixed positions, and no individual self. All concepts proposed by the sages can be regarded as statements existing on the same plane rather than prior or posterior.

5.0 Objective Knowledge about Chinese Cultural Heritage

Because Western philosophy is deduced via dialectical reasoning on the basis of certain prior concepts, philosophers may develop philosophies on the basis of different presumptions. Therefore, there is a history of development in Western philosophy. The explanations for certain things in a given domain made by different philosophers are often progressive, evolving step by step. In contrast to this, there is no history of wisdom. Nobody can write a history of the development of wisdom. A sage may say different words from different perspectives, but what he says represents an entire self-contained unit of wisdom, which could be interpreted again and again.

In order to think dialectically, Western philosophy requires a clear definition for each core concept, so that one can use them to recognize the external world. Philosophers can use various methods to examine the correctness of a proposition about objects in a given domain in order to approach the so-called "truth." By contrast, sage wisdom is expressed in the form of sayings without fixed definitions. These can remind people to see through the "Dao" (way) of ordinary things or events that is otherwise frequently taken for granted. An individual may be inclined to ignore the Dao because his sights are so obscured by prejudice that he can see only one side of the issue. A sage's words of wisdom may enable him to become aware (*Wu*, enlighten) of the entirety of things or events rather than learning a new framework for knowing the world.

Using Jullien's distinction between philosophy and wisdom, we can see the essential difference between traditional Chinese and modern Western culture. In my book *Knowledge and Action* (Hwang 1995), I pointed out that one of the major purposes of Western philosophy is to pursue objective knowledge, whereas that of Chinese philosophy is to provide practical wisdom. Despite the essential difference, it is possible for Chinese social scientists to construct objective knowledge about Chinese traditional culture by various methods as long as they are familiar with Western philosophy of science.

5.1 Two Perspectives of Culture

Understanding why I decided to construct the scientific microworld of Confucian cultural heritage, we are ready to answer some crucial questions proposed by Allwood (2018) about the definition of culture. He indicated that, "a challenge for the IPs is to coordinate what they mean by culture with the goals for their IP," and his review of previous IP literature indicated that, "focusing on meaning contents, definitions of culture range from treating culture as quite abstract, essentialist, and unchanging, to viewing culture as more interactive and dynamically changing" (p. 41).

In terms of this article, the perspective of treating culture as quite abstract, essentialist, and unchanging is following the approach of cultural psychologists who conceptualize culture as artifacts or man-made objects:

> [We] think of culture as a dynamically changing environment that is trans-formed by the artifacts created by prior generations ... [A]n artifact is an aspect of the material world that has been modified over the history of its incorporation into goal-directed human thought and action ... simulta-neously ideal (conceptual) and material. It is material in that it is embodied in physical form, whether in the morphology of a spoken, written or signed world, a ritual, or an artistic creation, or as a solid object like a pencil. It is ideal in that this material form has been shaped by historical participation in (successful, adaptive) human activities ... [C]ulture can be seen as the medium of human development which [prepares humans] for interaction with the world. (Cole & Parker, 2011: p. 135)

The perspective of treating culture as "more interactive and dynamically changing" is adopted by most cognitive psychologists who are conducting empirical research in the field of cross-cultural psychology:

> We define culture as *networks of knowledge* consisting of learned routines of thinking, as feeling, and interacting with other people, as well as a corpus of substantive assertions and ideas about aspects of the world . . . [C]ulture . . . is (a) shared . . . among a collection of interconnected individuals who are often demarcated by race, ethnicity, or nationality; (b) externalized by rich symbols, artifacts, social constructions, and social institutions (e.g., cultural icons, advertisements and news media); (c) used to form the common ground for communication among members; (d) transmitted from one generation to the next . . . ; and (e) undergoing continuous modifications. (Hong, 2009: p. 4)

In this definition, (a) belongs to the second perspective, but the author also recognized the existence and importance of the first perspective of culture in her statements (b), (c), (d), and (e). By the same token, the definition of culture is the one by Berry and Triandis (2006): "First, culture emerges in adaptive interactions between human and environments. Second, culture consists of shared elements. Third, culture is transmitted across time periods and generations" (p. 50).

5.2 Analytical Dualism

These two perspectives of culture should be discussed in terms of the analytical dualism proposed by Archer (1996), who argued that though culture, society, and agent are in fact inseparable, social scientists must treat them as analytically separable. The concepts utilized in such an analytical distinction will urge a researcher to consider the substantial difference between culture and social structure, to examine the interaction between them so as to understand the distinction between cultural ideas and material interests.

According to Archer (1996), because units for analyzing social structure such as role, organization, and institution can be differentiated easily, in contrast to this, most sociological theories tend to grasp culture by intuition without analysis. The ambiguity of the definition of culture can be traced to the myth of cultural integration prevailing in early literatures of anthropology.

The myth promotes a perspective that culture is shared by the whole community at the level of socio-cultural interaction (S-C interaction), and provides a theoretical ground for psychologists to develop scales or questionnaires to "measure" or "investigate" culture:

> [A] pattern of shared attitudes, beliefs, categorizations, self-definitions, norms, role definitions, and values that is organized around a theme that can be identified among those who speak a particular language, during

a specific historical period, and in a definable geographic region. (Triandis, 1996: p. 408)

The fallacy of conflation may hinder not only the analysis of interaction between these two levels, but also the eliding of cultural meanings at the cultural system level (CS) in social theorizing (Archer, 2005). When culture and agency are conflated, no analytical distinction is made between the "parts of culture" and the "people"; this fallacy of conflation prevents the analysis of their interplay from being the foundation of cultural dynamics (Archer, 1996). Consequently, there is no source of internal cultural dynamics available to explain social change. Accordingly, sources of change are said to be externally located (Archer, 2005). Therefore, Archer proposed that an analytic distinction should be made between CS and S-C.

5.2.1 Cultural System and Socio-cultural Interaction

As Allwood (2018) showed in his literature review, IR researchers all over the world have proposed various definitions of culture with a consideration of their own problematic situation. The concepts of culture as defined by IP researchers oscillate between these two levels of analysis. For instance, when culture was defined as "cultural heritage" (e.g., Hwang, 2006), "a rubric of patterned variables" (Kim & Park, 2006), "the collective utilization of nature and human resources to achieve desired outcomes" (Kim, 2001: p. 58), or "a body of collectively shared values, principles, practices, customs, and tradition" (Dudgeon, 2017: p. 320), it was conceptualized as something like a cultural system. As Allwood (2018) noted, Kim and Park's (2006) definition of culture allows for change: "The culture that people have built for themselves can have a different meaning for their children and their children may modify the culture" (Kim & Park, 2006: p. 36), in fact meaning socio-cultural interaction.

Allwood (2018) is correct in saying, "Similar to this, but possibly still more essentialist, is the cultural concept promoted in different texts by Hwang. In Hwang's view the central part of culture consists of 'cultural heritage' (that is, very slowly changing tradition)" (p. 41). However, he did not indicate that indigenous psychologists should construct scientific microworlds of culture-inclusive theories to tell people what is their cultural heritage.

5.2.2 Morphostasis of Cultural System

According to Archer's (1996) proposal of analytic dualism, a cultural system is a result of real human products, comprising all proposed ideas knowable at any one time that may be true or false (Archer & Elder-Vass, 2012: p. 95). It is constituted by the corpus of existing intelligibilia (i.e., by all things capable of being grasped, deciphered, understood, or known by someone). "By definition the cultural intelligibilia form a system, for all items must be expressed in a common language (or be translated in principle) since it is a precondition of their being intelligible" (p. 104).

Archer and Elder-Vass (2012) proposed that a viable theoretical approach to both culture and structure ought to include diachronic as well as synchronic analysis. The former would examine how certain ideas came to prevail at a certain time, who advocated them, and why and what challenges these ideas have encountered both in the past and at present. The latter would aim to understand what sustains morphostasis or cultural reproduction rather than morphogenesis or transformation over time (cf. Archer, 1996: p. 290). The morphostasis of a given culture as shown by such a scientific microworld is abstract, essentialist, and unchanging, while the morphogenesis of that cultural heritage in people's lifeworlds is more interactive and dynamically changing.

Therefore, it is necessary for IPs to make a distinction between scientific microworld and lifeworld. When I said, "As people of a given culture contemplate the nature of the universe and the situation of mankind, they gradually formulate their worldviews with original thinking over the course of their history" (Hwang, 2011c: p. 128), I meant people in their lifeworlds, but not scientific microworld. When I argued that cultures have deep structures, although people may be unaware of these deep structures, they can be made explicit by taking a structural perspective (Hwang, 2006), I meant the construction of culture-inclusive theories, Therefore, I concluded that among the important goals for indigenization of psychology in east Asian cultures is to ascertain the deep structure of various cultural traditions. As shown in Figure 4.1, structuralism is used to link the deep structure of a given cultural tradition and the surface structure when it was manifested in people's lifeworlds.

5.2.3 The "What" Question and "How"

Though I have devoted myself to the indigenization movement of psychology for more than twenty years, the significance of my approach has attracted more and more attention recently in light of the rise of China. Social scientists are aware of a rapid growth of necessity for understanding Confucian cultural heritage when discussing various social problems in China. For instance, in an international conference on *Confucianism, Democracy and Constitutionalism: Global and East Asian Perspectives* held in Taipei, Taiwan, the well-respected sinologist Roger T. Ames (2013) presented an article titled "Confucian Role Ethics and Deweyan Democracy: A Challenge to the Ideology of Individualism" in which he indicated:

> Framing our question as "What is Confucianism?" in analytical terms tends to essentialize Confucianism as a specific ideology – a technical philosophy – that can be stipulated with varying degrees of detail and accuracy. What is a question that is perhaps more successfully directed at attempts at systematic philosophy where through analysis one can seed to abstract the formal, cognitive structure in the language of principles, theories, and concepts. However, the what question is at best a first step in evaluating the content and worth of a holistic and thus fundamentally aesthetic tradition that takes as its basic premise the uniqueness of each and every situation, and in which the goal of ritualized living is to redirect attention back to the level of concrete feeling. Beyond the "what" question, we need to ask more importantly after the always transforming and reforming content of a still persistent tradition: How has "Confucianism" functioned historically generation after generation within the specific conditions of an evolving Chinese culture to try to make the most of its circumstances? (Ames, 2013: pp. 20–21)

It seems to me that such a question as "What is Confucianism?" should be answered by constructing culture-inclusive theories on various aspects of Confucian morphostasis. If and only if we are able to construct culture-inclusive theories to illustrate the morphostasis of Confucianism at the cultural system level, can we answer such questions as "How has Confucianism functioned historically generation after generation?" by studying its morphogenesis at a particular point in time and space.

5.3 Confucian Ethics for Ordinary People

In chapter 5 of my book *Foundations of Chinese Psychology* (Hwang, 2012), I used the *Face and Favor* model as a framework for analyzing the inner structure of Confucianism. My analysis is the corpus of sayings by pre-Qin Confucianists. Analyzing the inner structure of Confucian thoughts by using the theoretical model of *Face and Favor* as a framework of reference enables us to construct a series of culture-inclusive theories to represent the culture system or morphostasis of pre-Qin Confucianism as advocated by the philosophy of analytical dualism (Archer, 1996). The results of analysis showed that pre-Qin Confucianism contained four major parts:

1. Confucian conceptions of destiny
2. Confucian theory of self-cultivation with the Way of Humanity
3. Confucian ethics for ordinary people
4. Confucian ethics for scholars: contributing to the world with the Way of Humanity

Confucians of the pre-Qin period classified two categories of ethics for interpersonal relationship arrangement, namely, ethics for ordinary people and ethics for scholars. The former should be followed by everyone, including scholars. Because *Foundations of Chinese Psychology* focuses on the study of interpersonal relations among ordinary people in Chinese society, here I will focus on the Confucian ethics for ordinary people.

5.3.1 Ethical System of Benevolence, Righteousness, and Propriety

The Doctrine of the Mean (*Zhongyung,* 中庸) was said to be works completed by Confucian scholars during the Han dynasty (206 BC–200 AD) and Zisi (子思), a grandson of Confucius. It seems to me that the following passage from *Zhongyung* can best depict the relations among three key concepts in Confucian ethics for ordinary people, namely benevolence (仁, *ren*), righteousness (義, *yi*), and propriety (禮, *li*):

> Benevolence (*ren*) is the characteristic attribute of personhood. The first priority of its expression is showing affection to those closely related to us. Righteousness (*yi*) means appropriateness, respecting the superior is its most important rule. Loving others according to who they are, and respecting superiors according to their ranks gives rise to the forms and distinctions of propriety (*li*) in social life. (Zhongyung, ch. 20)

The idea of loving others according to their relationships with us and respecting superiors according to their rank indicates an emphasis on the differential order of interpersonal relationships. Such an abstract statement is relatively unusual in Classical pre-Qin Confucian works. This citation from *Zhongyung* not only demonstrates the interrelated concepts of benevolence (*ren*), righteousness (*yi*), and propriety (*li*), but also implies two dimensions along which Confucians assessed role relationships in social interaction.

5.3.2 Transcendental Formal Structure

Confucian ethics for ordinary people can be interpreted in terms of Western justice theory. In Western social psychology, the concept of justice in human society is classified into two categories: procedural justice and distributive justice. Procedural justice refers to the procedures to be followed by members of a group to determine methods of resource distribution. Distributive justice is the particular method of distribution that is accepted by members of that group (Leventhal, 1976, 1980).

Confucius advocated that procedural justice in social interaction should be based on the principle of respecting superiors, meaning that the role of resource

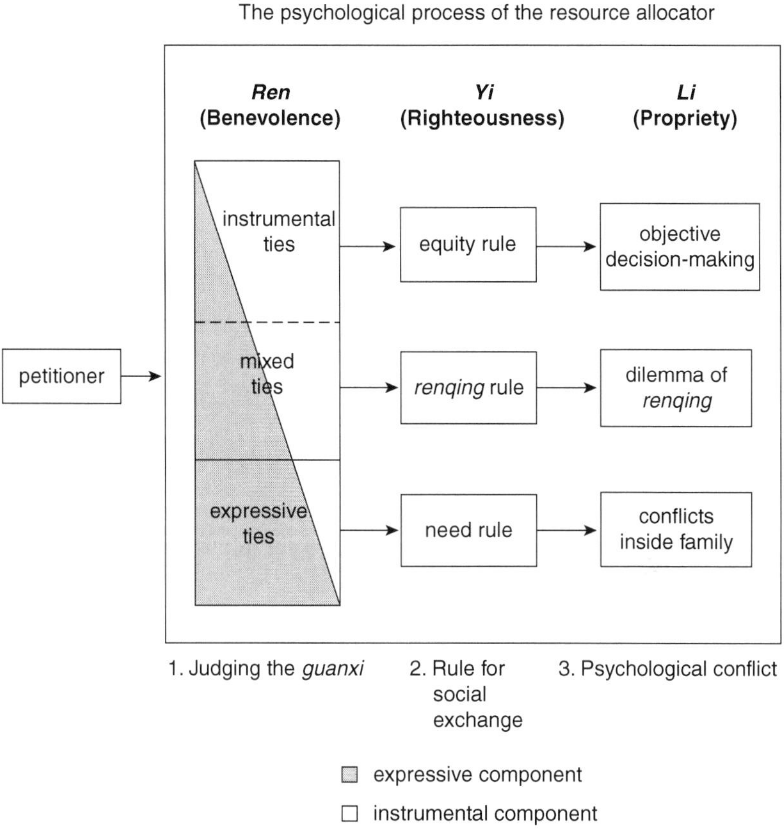

The psychological process of the resource allocator

Figure 5.1 The Confucian ethical system of benevolence–righteousness–propriety (adapted from Hwang, 1995: p. 233)

allocator should be played by the person who occupies the superior position. The resource allocator should follow the principle of favoring the intimate in choosing an appropriate method for distributive justice. In other words, for Confucian followers, it is righteous to determine who has decision-making power by calling on the principle of respecting superiors, and it is also righteous for the resource allocator to distribute resources in accordance with the principle of favoring the intimate.

It should be emphasized that the *Confucian ethical system of benevolence–righteousness–propriety* as shown in Figure 5.1 is isomorphic to the psychological process of resource allocator in the model of *Face and Favor* as shown in Figure 4.1. Therefore, the Confucian ethical system is the transcendental formal structure for sustaining the lifeworlds of the Chinese people, and might be applied in any kind of social interaction with other parties of various relationships. Moreover, the Confucian concept of *yi* (righteousness) is frequently translated into English as justice. However, inasmuch as *yi* is usually used in connection with other Chinese characters like *ren-yi* (literally, benevolent righteousness or benevolent justice) or *qing-yi* (literally, affective righteousness or affective justice), it should be noted that the meaning of this term is completely different from the concept of universal justice in Western culture (Rawls, 1971).

5.3.3 Substantial Ethical Values

Emphasizing the principle of respecting the superior in procedural justice and the principle of favoring the intimate in distributive justice constitutes the formal structure of Confucian ethics for ordinary people. Although this transcendental formal structure manifests itself in many types of interpersonal relationships, Confucians also make substantial ethical demands for certain relationships. Confucians have established five cardinal ethics for the five major dyadic relationships in Chinese society, proposing that the social interaction between members of each pair should be constructed on the basis of the *Way of Humanity* (天道). The fact that each of the roles or functions in these five cardinal relationships is distinctive indicates that the core values that should be emphasized in each are also different:

> Between father and son, there should be affection (親); between sovereign and subordinate, righteousness (義); between husband and wife, attention to their separate functions (別); between elder brother and younger, a proper order (序); and between friends, trustworthiness (信). (*The Works of Mencius*, ch. 3A: Duke Wen of Teng)

In the aforementioned passage, affection (親), righteousness (義), separate functions (別), proper order (序), and trustworthiness (信) are substantial ethical values for regulating dyad interactions of the five cardinal relationships advocated by Mencius. Three of these five cardinal rules were designed for regulating interpersonal relationships within the family (expressive ties). The other two relationships – friends and sovereign/subordinate – are relations of mixed ties. It should also be noted that, except for the relationship between friends, the remaining four relationships are vertical ones between superiors and inferiors.

5.3.4 Nature of Human Beings

After the death of Confucius, Mencius (who lived during the pre-Qin period) engaged in several debates with his opponents about human nature. In his dialogue with Gongduzi (公都子), Mencius proposed his famous sayings about the Four Origins (四端) in answering Gongduzi's question:

When I say human beings are inherently good, I am talking about their most fundamental qualities of feeling. If some do evil, it is not the fault of their natural endowment.

Everyone has the feeling of concern for the wellbeing of others.
Everyone has the sense of shame and disgust at their own evil.
Everyone has the sense to treat others respectfully.
Everyone has the sense to judge right and wrong.
The feeling of concern for the wellbeing of others is Benevolence (仁, ren).
The sense of shame and disgust is Righteousness (義, yi).
The sense to treat others respectfully is Propriety (禮, li).
The sense to judge right and wrong is Wisdom (智, zhi).
Benevolence, Righteousness, Propriety and Wisdom are not melded into us from outside. They are our original endowment. You have not really thought them through yet!
Hence it is said: "If you strive for it, you will attain it; if you ignore it, you will lose it." Men are different in their extents of actualization. Some are double, some fivefold are, and some manifest it to an incalculable degree, because some are not able to fully develop their natural endowments. (Mencius, *Gaozi*, part I, ch. 6)

In addition to these positive statements, Mencius also argued for his sayings of the Four Origins with more assertive modes of negative statements to defend his position that the four virtues of Benevolence, Righteousness, Propriety, and Wisdom are essential to human beings (See Mencius, *Gongsun Cheu,* part I, ch. 6). Many Confucian scholars had tried to expound the meaning of these origins from various perspectives, but it is very difficult to explain the relations among those four concepts without a theoretical construction for illustrating the nature of human beings.

5.3.5 Second-Order Morality

Conceiving Mencius' discourse on the Four Origins in the context of my theoretical construction, benevolence (*ren*), righteousness (*yi*), and propriety (*li*) can be explained in the context of Confucian ethics for ordinary people (Figure 5.1), while wisdom (智, *zhi*) is located in the Mandala model of self (Figure 4.2). In his book *Relational Being: Beyond Self and Community*, Gergen (2009) classified morality into two categories:First-order morality has meaning in a certain style of life: it consists of values for constituting long-lasting patterns of relationships, is implicit and existing everywhere, but has nothing to do with good or evil. An individual may utilize it to integrate various ideas about one's personhood to formalize his personal identity; he or she may also use it to constitute social identity in a given social group. First-order morality may change from an implicit state into second-order morality, which can be explicitly stated as a set of norms, rules, or principles. This situation usually happens when two cultural groups encounter and are in value conflict with each other.

In terms of Gergen's (2009) classification, wisdom (*zhi*) is the first-order morality, which can be used flexibly to deal with any situation of social interaction. One's reflection on an entire problematic situation may become second-order morality of benevolence (*ren*), righteousness (*yi*), and propriety (*li*), which can be stated explicitly as norms, rules, or principles.

5.3.6 Modal of Five Virtues

After the destruction caused by the First Emperor of Qin's burning books and burying intellectuals alive, the Martial Emperor of Han dynasty (156–87 BC) adopted Dong Zhongshu's (董仲舒 179–104 BC) proposal of promoting only Confucianism and dismissing other schools of thought. Dong also proposed his famous saying of Three Bonds and expanded Mencius' discourse on Four Origins into Five Virtues, namely, benevolence (*ren*), righteousness (*yi*), propriety (*li*), wisdom (*zhi*), and trustworthiness (信, *xin*), which signifies the accomplishment of Confucian theorization on relationalism.

Following the reasoning I have presented, a model of Five Virtues can be constructed to depict the ideal dyad interaction of Confucianism (see Figure 5.2), which must be elaborated in more detail. Most dialogues between Confucius and his disciples as recorded in the *Analects* involved questions by disciples that were answered by Confucius. However, those sayings actively mentioned by Confucius may reflect the core values of Confucianism:

> The Master said, "Shen, my doctrine is that of an all prevailing unity."
> The disciple Zeng replied, "Yes."
> The Master went out. The other disciples asked, "What does his saying mean?"

> Zeng seng said, "The doctrine of our master is just 忠 (zhong, literary loyalty) and 恕 (shu, literary forgiveness), and nothing more."

In accordance with Zhu Xi's annotation, *Zhong* (忠) means to be authentic to one's best effort (盡己), while *shu* (恕) means the benevolent exercise of it to others (推己及人). Conceiving this in the context of the model of Five Virtues for dyad interaction (see Figure 5.2), when *yin* and *yang* components of the *Taiji* represent two parties of interaction, the characters *zhong* (忠) and *shu* (恕) within the small circles of the two components imply that, when one of the two parties is exercising authentic benevolence in dealing with its opposite, the other party will repay and treat the first party in the same way. Both parties are

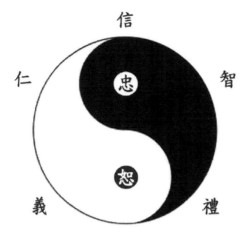

Figure 5.2 The model of Five Virtues for dyad interaction.

acting in congruence with the ethical codes of benevolence-righteousness-propriety, so the virtue of trustworthiness (信) may emerge as a consequence of their interaction. Therefore, the character信 is located at the top of *Taiji* for dyad interaction.

5.3.7 Three Bonds and Ten Forms of Righteousness

In addition to the ideas discussed above, Dong Zhongshu also proposed the idea of the *Three Bonds* (*sangang*), which had been frequently and closely linked to *Five Virtues* (*wuchang*). However, the Three Bonds delineated the absolute authority of the ruler over the minister, the father over the son, and the husband over the wife. Under the influence of the Three Bonds, some Han scholars further advocated the idea of the *Ten Forms of Righteousness* (十義).

> What are the things which humans consider righteous (*yi*)? Kindness on the part of the father, and filial duty on that of the son; gentleness on the part of the elder brother, and obedience on that of the younger; righteousness on the part of the husband, and submission on that of the wife; kindness on the part of the elders, and deference on that of juniors; benevolence on the part of the ruler, and loyalty on that of the minister. These are the ten things that humans consider to be right.

As I indicated before, the substantial ethical values for each of the five cardinal relationships (五倫) might be changed from time to time, depending on the atmosphere of social context. The *Book of Rites* (禮記, *Liji*) contains many works composed by Confucian scholars during the Han dynasty. For the sake of transforming Confucianism into the orthodox state philosophy for the

Han Empire, the ten items of righteousness are specifically defined in the *Liji* such that there exists a differential order within the five sets of roles involved. In accordance with the Ten Forms of Righteousness (*yi*), fathers, elder brothers, husbands, the elderly, or rulers should make decisions in line with the principles of kindness, gentleness, righteousness, kindness, and benevolence, respectively. As for sons, younger brothers, wives, juniors, or ministers, the principles of filial duty, obedience, submission, deference, and loyalty should apply.

5.3.8 Absolute Authority of Three Bonds

Based on the deep structure of ethics for ordinary people, Mencius proposed five cardinal ethics with the core value of benevolence (*ren*), requesting each party to fulfill its role obligations in dyad interactions (i.e., the five significant relationships) in the lifeworld. Nevertheless, the ideas of Three Bonds or Ten Forms of Righteousness imply power domination of absolute authority, and have exerted a profound negative influence over Chinese culture in general.

From the modernist point of view, the Three Bonds and Ten Forms of Righteousness are primarily based on power and domination; such exploitative relationships can hardly be redeemable as either social or family ethics. Therefore, Tu (1998) suggested that it is necessary to differentiate and to study the complex interaction between the authoritarianism of the Three Bonds and the benevolence of the five cardinal ethics at the cultural system level. As the politicized Confucian ideology of control, the institution of Three Bonds was a deliberate attempt to utilize Confucian values for the maintenance of a specific social order. This has proven detrimental to human flourishing. On the contrary, the five cardinal ethics deliberated by Mencius with the idea of self-cultivation are not only compatible with but also essential to personal growth. Therefore, he argued that a sophisticated critique of the Three Bonds must involve adequate appreciation of the Mencian conception of the five cardinal ethics.

5.4 Procedure of Theoretical Construction

In her keynote speech presented at the 1999 AASP Conference at Academia Sinica, Taipei, Taiwan, Greenfield (2000) delivered the following statement:

> The incorporation of culture into mainstream psychology will not come from simply presenting data on group differences, no matter how exciting or dramatic these differences may be. My most important theoretical mission is to introduce the idea of a deep structure of culture. As in language, deep structure of culture generates behaviors and interpretations of human

behavior in an infinite array of domains and situations. I believe that the concepts behind individualism and collectivism, independence and interdependence, a relational vs. an individual orientation and so on are all indexing a common deep structure. (p. 229)

I strongly agree with Greenfield's arguments.

5.4.1 The Deep Structure of Culture

From the perspective of structuralism (Lévi-Strauss, 1976), all human activities, including cognitions as well as actions, result from simulating various relations in nature. Nature is a system with steady, unchangeable, and mutually linked relations among its various components. As a part of nature, from generation to generation people have gradually developed various sets of customs in their lifeworlds that are congruent with the natural order. These customs, rites, and various forms of life are the consequences of routinization, crystallization, or systematization of human practices in simulation of nature. For the sake of survival and prosperity, human rationality has to handle the various events encountered in a person's lifeworld so as to adjust to the environment. The diversified social phenomena seen in a given society are manifested from an undetectable underlying structure that originated from the inherited capability of the human mind.

These structures are the unconscious models of human rationality, which are a kind of autonomous model followed by human thinking. All of the empirical facts in human social life are a result of the arrangement and combination of these models. The human capability to simulate nature is manifest in the customs and social relationships of premodern civilization. The more advanced the society, the more progressive the civilization, the more complicated the social relationships. Many linkages among people depart from the natural order, which makes recognition of the original appearance of some premodern civilizations difficult. The goal of structuralism is to reveal the fundamental structure of cultural relations that might be very complicated in appearance.

5.4.2 From Unconscious to Conscious Model

From the perspective of structuralism, both the language games played by people in their lifeworlds and the microworlds of knowledge constructed by scientists have their own structures. But there are tremendous differences between these two kinds of structure. In terms of Piaget's (1972) genetic epistemology, the structure of scientific knowledge is a *conscious* model constructed with formal operational thinking by an individual scientist with fully developed intelligence. In contrast, the language games played by people in their lifeworlds are constituted by the rationality of a cultural group under the influence of their collective unconscious over the history of their evolution. These language games originate from the deep structure of the culture, which is an *unconscious* model. People are unaware of it directly in their daily lives, but researchers may reveal the deep structure using the methods of structuralism.

From the viewpoint of constructive realism, the theoretical models of *Face and Favor* and *Confucian ethics for ordinary people* discussed in the previous subsections are both microworlds constructed by social scientists. Culture groups create the deep structure of their culture unconscious of rationality, but the structure cannot be recognized intuitively through the rationality of ordinary people. The structure can only be recognized when revealed and reinterpreted by a researcher.

As soon as the unconscious model has been revealed by a social scientist, it can be reasonably assumed that the model can be applied to various cultures. For instance, in his book *Structures of Social Life*, Alan P. Fiske (1991) classified elementary forms of social behavior into four main categories: communal sharing, equality matching, market pricing, and authority ranking.

5.4.3 Isomorphism

A comparison between my theoretical *Face and Favor* model and these four modes reveals that authority ranking is implied in the relationship between petitioner and resource allocator, and the relationships of communal sharing, equality matching, and market pricing, respectively, correspond to expressive ties, mixed ties, instrumental ties and their related rules of exchange in my model.

By the same token, comparing Fiske's four modes of interpersonal relationships with *Confucian ethics for ordinary people*, it can be seen that the procedural justice of respecting the superior corresponds to the concept of authority ranking, while the Confucian distributive justice of favoring the intimate corresponds to other modes of interpersonal relationships such as communal sharing, equality matching, and market pricing.

From the perspective of constructive realism (Wallner, 1994; Wallner & Jandl, 2006), the theoretical *Face and Favor* model constructed on the basis of social exchange theory can be stratified to the four elementary forms of interpersonal relationships proposed by Fiske (1991, 1992). It is applicable to other cultures as well. Using the linguistic records in Confucian scriptures to analyze the deep structure of Confucianism, it is clear that the theoretical *Face and Favor* model and *Confucian ethics for ordinary people* are isomorphic to each other. Nevertheless, linguistic analysis reveals the specific features of interpersonal relationships in Confucian societies.

5.4.4 Cultural Hybridity or Isolation

The distinction between lifeworld and scientific microworld of deep structure or generative mechanisms can be used to resolve the controversial issues relating to cultural *hybridity* or *isolation* (Allwood, 2018: p. 52–55). When culture is defined as "the very fiber of our being–all that we sense, feel, believe, value, think and do" (Sundararajan, Kim, & Park, 2017: p. 5), it means culture in one's lifeworld. For most individuals in the contemporary world, "even before the era of globalization *no* culture exists in its pure form" (Sundararajan, Misra, & Marsella, 2013: p. 70).

In terms of the Mandala model of self, culture may provide an indication of what is worth noticing and worth pursuing in the world and assumes "causal autonomy" by influencing "what people want" to be a *person* and "what they want " as an *individual* in a particular situation (Vaisey, 2010). In order to understand how culture affects individual and collective action, Abramson (2012) reviewed works in disciplines of modern social science such as sociology, anthropology, and political science, and constructed a context-dependent model of culture in action, in which he introduced the term "cultural input" of wisdom-related knowledge to refer to a wider set of attributions that may organize the complete sequences of actions while still pointing toward a preferred outcome in one's lifeworld (see Figure 4.2).

In other words, the external social environment people are in, or one's lifeworld, can cause them to activate repertoires from different culture stored in their memory (Weber & Morris, 2010). The fact that "cultural influence on individuals is partial and plural and cultural traditions interact and change each other" might be termed as *polyculturalism* (Morris, Chiu, & Liu, 2015: p. 634) or cultural *hybridity* (Allwood, 2018).

5.4.5 Multiculturalism

But here I would like to indicate that the antithesis of *polyculturalism* is not the so-called *culturalism* that argues that "individuals are shaped by one primary culture and the world's cultural traditions are separate and independent" (Morris, Chiu, & Lin, 2015: p. 633). It should be *multiculturalism* as advocated by Canadian philosopher Charles Taylor (1992), which means that the cultural systems of morality in each society are different from one another and should be studied independently as a scientific microworld.

In his masterpiece *Sources of the Self: The Making of Modern Identity,* Taylor (1989) argued that insofar as we are able to construct morality of a given culture into a well-organized cultural system, it may become a system of *constitutive goods* that might have a better chance to compete with other foreign systems of morality and to become *hyper goods*. Otherwise, it will stay at the level of *life goods*, prevailing in people's lifeworld only.

This is the main reason why I have spent more than forty years in developing my epistemological strategy of cultural analysis and utilized it to construct culture-inclusive theories. As I indicated in previous sections of this Element, the *Confucian ethical system of benevolence (ren)–righteousness (yi)–propriety (li) for ordinary people* is the transcendental formal structure for sustaining Chinese social structure which will be manifested in various aspects of Chinese social life. When an observed phenomenon cannot be explained by imported Western theory, it is necessary for indigenous psychologists to construct a new theory to account for that phenomenon. In this situation, the aforementioned *Confucian ethical system of benevolence–righteousness–propriety* can be used as a foundation for constructing new theories. The rational can be explained in terms of philosophy of science.

5.4.6 Model of Covering Law

Scientists construct theories because they want to explain observed phenomena. In his *Aspects of Scientific Explanation,* Hempel (1965) proposed a *model of covering law*, which stated that scientific explanation usually contains two kinds of statements – general laws and antecedent conditions (see Figure 5.3). Using these two kinds of *explanans* as the premises, a scientist can deduct a description of a phenomenon, which is called the *explanandum*.

Hempel (1965) advocated that the *deductive model* can be used for either explanation or prediction in scientific research. If a scientist observes a phenomenon (E) first, then tries to propose general laws (L) and antecedent conditions (C) for its occurrence, this is scientific *explanation*. In contrast to

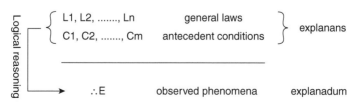

Figure 5.3 A model of covering law

this, if the scientist knows general laws (L) and antecedent conditions (C), and tries to devise from them a description about a phenomenon, then it is *prediction*.

Viewed from the perspective of the deductive model or model of covering law, when a psychologist conducts empirical research by either the imposed etic or derived etic approach, and finds that many of their research findings cannot be adequately explained by their theory, they must reflect that most Western theories have been constructed on the presumption of individualism, but Chinese society has been constructed on the basis of Confucian relationism (Hwang, 2000).

As I indicated at the beginning of this section, the mechanism of *Confucian ethics for ordinary people* (see, Figure 5.1) developed as the deep structure of Confucianism (Hwang, 2001). The operation of this mechanism can be transformed into a set of high probability propositions that may be viewed as the *hard core* in Lakatos' scientific research program, or the *general law* in Hempel's model of covering law.

5.4.7 Scientific Research Program

Lakatos advocated for the philosophy of *sophisticated falsificationism* in opposition to Popper's *naïve falsificationism* (Lakatos, 1970), and argued that scientists would not easily give up the propositions of a scientific theory once they are falsified by empirical research as Popper predicted. In accordance with Lakatos's philosophy, when an imported Western theory T fails in predicting local phenomena and encounters anomalies, an indigenous researcher has to assume the task of constructing a new theory T' with a careful consideration of the antecedent conditions and adding the auxiliary hypotheses.

For a naïve falsificationist, when a proposition stating empirical research findings is in conflict with the theoretical hypothesis to be tested, the hypothesis is said to be falsified. For sophisticated falsificationists, a scientific theory T is falsified if and only if an alternative new theory T' is characterized with the following features:

1. T' accounts for more empirical facts than T;
2. T' shares the previous success of T, all the irrefutable contents of T can be covered by T';
3. Compared with T, T' enables scientists to make more predictions that can be corroborated by empirical observation and experimentation.

In other words, to falsify an old theory, a scientist has to be familiar with not only the methodology of hypothesis testing, but also the philosophy of constructing a competitive alternative theory. However, a scientific theory does not exist in isolation, but as part of a series of tightly interconnected theories. Thus, Lakatos proposed *sophisticated falsificationism* and suggested that the basic unit for examination in scientific research is neither a particular scientific proposition, nor an isolated theory, but rather a series of theories or a scientific research program. The durability of scientific theory and its succession can be understood only when a series of scientific theories or a scientific research program has been taken into consideration.

6 Conclusion

Following this approach, a series of culture-inclusive theories can be constructed to constitute the scientific microworld of Confucian relationism (Hwang, 2012). This epistemological strategy can be used not only in the field of psychology, but also in other fields of social science, including sociology, anthropology, counseling, education, management, criminology, and so on.

6.1 Independent Tradition of Social Sciences

Now we have organized a *Chinese Association of Indigenous Social Sciences* to promote this approach in both Taiwan and mainland China. We are trying to educate our members, particularly young scholars and Ph.D. students, to be familiar with philosophy of science and use this epistemological strategy to conduct theoretical or empirical research. Some of their works were published as a special issue in the international journal *Frontiers in Psychology* (Hwang, Shiah, & Yit, 2017).

I agree with Pe-Pua, cited in the conclusion of Allwood's (2018: p. 56) monograph:

> the development of IP in various countries [shows that] there is no single path for developing IP. Each country has their particularities in terms of national history, policies, priorities, and positioning in the academic environment.

I have confidence that my approach will become very popular among the Chinese academic community of social science in the coming years when they are eager to establish their own tradition of independent social science, as well as their intellectual identity as a consequence of the rise of China. Psychologists in other countries may or may not be interested in this approach because their social environments and historical conditions are very different from China, even though my universal models and epistemological strategy might also be applicable to other societies.

6.2 The Instrumental Value of IP

Allwood (2018) also mentioned an interesting point about the future of IP: Michael H. Bond's (2010) *Oxford Handbook of Chinese Psychology* does not relate to IP and the book's index does not include the phrase "indigenous psychology" or the term "indigenous." This is a matter of course, and not surprising. As I noted earlier, indigenous psychology is, in fact, a kind of cultural psychology. The term "indigenization of psychology" implies that it is an academic movement seeking a philosophical foundation for future development. The search might cease as soon as an effective epistemological strategy has been clearly identified, unless a more efficient strategy can be found to compete with it. Because the movement was prompted by implementation of the Western research paradigm, the term "indigenization" seems adequate to describe the process of IP researchers who have to construct culture-inclusive theories to compete with the foreign ones.

The final achievement of all those epistemological works may be to make substantial contributions to the growth of culture psychology. Therefore, the term "indigenous" in contemporary "indigenous psychology" has *instrumental* value only, not *terminal* value. Both terms might become obsolete if the final goal of a full-fledged independent social science can be established.

References

Abramson, C. A. (2012). From "either-or" to "when and how": A context-dependent model of culture in action. *Journal for the Theory of Social Behaviour, 42*(2): 155–180.

Adair, J. G. (1996). The indigenous psychology bandwagon: Cautions and considerations. In J. Pandey, D. Sinha, & D. P. S. Bhawuk (Eds.), In *Asian contributions to cross-cultural psychology*, 50–58. New Delhi: Sage.

Adair, J. G. (2006). Creating indigenous psychologies: Insights from empirical social studies of the science of psychology. In U. Kim, K.-S. Yang, & K.- K. Hwang (Eds.), *Indigenous and cultural psychology: Understanding people in context* (pp. 467–485). New York: Springer.

Adair, J. G., Puhan, B. N., & Vohra, N. (1993). Indigenization of psychology: Empirical assessment of progress in Indian research. *International Journal of Psychology, 28*, 149–169.

Allwood, C. M. (2013). The role of culture and understanding in research. *Social Epistemology Review and Reply Collective, 2*(5): 1–11.

Allwood, C. M. (2018). *The nature and challenges of indigenous psychologies*. Cambridge: Cambridge University Press.

Ames, R. T. (2013). Confucian role ethics and Deweyan democracy: A challenge to the ideology of individualism. Presented at International Conference on Confucianism, Democracy and Constitutionalism: Global and East Asian Perspectives. Institute for Advanced studies in Humanities and Social Sciences, NTU, Taiwan.

Archer, M. S. (1996). *Culture and agency: The place of culture in social theory* (Revised edition). New York: Cambridge University Press.

Archer, M. S. (2005). Structure, culture and agency. In M. D. Jacobs & N. W. Hanrahan, (Eds.), *The Blackwell companion to the sociology of culture* (pp. 17–34). UK: Blackwell Publishing.

Archer, M. S. & Elder-Vass, D. (2012). Cultural system or norm circles? An exchange. *European Journal of Social Theory, 15*, 93–115.

Azuma, H. (1984). Psychology in a non-Western culture: the Philippines. *International Journal of Psychology, 19*(1–4): 45–55.

Baltes, P. B. & Kunzmann, U. (2004). Two faces of wisdom: Wisdom as a general theory of knowledge and judgment about excellence in mind and virtue vs. wisdom as everyday realization in people and products. *Human Development, 47*, 290–299.

Baltes, P. B., & Smith, J. (1990). Toward a psychology of wisdom and its ontogenesis. *Wisdom: Its Nature, Origins, and Development*, *1*, 87–120.

Baltes, P. B., Dittmann-Kohli, F., & Dixon, R. A. (1984). New perspectives on the development of intelligence in adulthood: Toward a dual-process conception and a model of selective optimization with compensation. *Life-Span Development and Behavior*, *6*, 33–76.

Basalla, G. (1967). The spread of western science. *Science*, *156*(3775): 611–622.

Berry, J. W. (1989). Imposed etics-emics-derived etics: The operationalization of a compelling idea. *International Journal of Psychology*, *24*, 721–735.

Berry, J. W., Poortinga, Y. H., Segall, M. H., & Dasen, P. R. (1992). *Cross-cultural psychology: Research and applications*. Cambridge: Cambridge University Press.

Berry, J. W., & Triandis, H. (2006). *Culture*. In K. Pawlik & G. d'Ydewalle (Eds.), *Psychological concepts: An international historical perspective* (pp.47–62). Hove: Psychology Press.

Bhaskar, R. A. (1975). *A realist theory of science*, London: Verso.

Bhaskar, R. A. (1978). *The possibility of naturalism*. Atlantic Highlands, NJ: Humanities Press.

Bond, M. H., (2010). *The Oxford handbook of Chinese psychology*. New York: Oxford University Press.

Bourdieu, P. (1990). *In other words: Essays towards a reflexive sociology*. Trans. by A. Mattew. Stanford: Stanford University Press.

Brubaker, R. (1984). *The limits of rationality: An essay on the social and moral thought of Max Weber*. London: George Allen & Unwin.

Clayton, V. P. (1982). Wisdom and intelligence: The nature and function of knowledge in the later years. *International Journal of Aging and Human Development*, *15*, 315–321.

Cole, M. (1996). *Cultural psychology: A once and future discipline*. Cambridge, MA: Harvard University Press.

Cole, M., & Parker, M. (2011). Culture and cognition. In K. D. Keith (Ed.), *Cross-cultural psychology: Contemporary themes and perspectives* (pp. 133–159). Chichester, UK: Wiley-Blackwell.

de Souza, D. E. (2014). Culture, context and society: The underexplored potential of critical realism as a philosophical framework for theory and practice. *Asian Journal of Social Psychology*, *17*(2): 141–151.

Dudgeon, P. (2017). Editorial Australian indigenous psychology. *Australian Psychologist*, *52*, 251–254.

Enriquez, V. (1977). Filipino psychology in the third world. *Philippine Journal of Psychology*, *10*, 3–18.

Enriquez, V. G. (1993). Developing a Filipino psychology. In U. Kim & J. W. Berry (Eds.), *Indigenous psychologies research and experience in cultural context* (pp. 152–169). Newbury Park: Sage Publications.

Evans-Pritchard, E. E. (1964). *Social anthropology and other essays.* New York: The Free Press.

Fiske, A. P. (1991). *Structures of social life: The four elementary forms of human relations.* New York: The Free Press.

Fiske, A. P. (1992). The four elementary forms of social life: Framework for a unified theory of social relations. *Psychological Review, 99,* 689–723.

Foucault, Michel (1966). *The order of things: An archaeology of the human sciences.* Trans. by A. Sheridan-Smith. New York: Random House.

Gergen, K. (2009). *Relational being: beyond self and community.* Oxford: Oxford University Press.

Giddens, A. (1984). *The constitution of society: Outline of the theory of structuration.* Berkeley: University of California Press.

Giddens, A. (1993). *New rules of sociological method: A positive critique of interpretative sociologies* (2nd ed.). Stanford: Stanford University Press.

Greenfield, P. M. (2000). Three approaches to the psychology of culture: Where do they come from? Where can they go? *Asian Journal of Social Psychology, 3*(3), 223–240.

Harris, G. G. (1989). Concepts of individual, self, and person in description and analysis. *American Anthropologist, 91,* 599–612.

Heidegger, M. (1966). *Discourse on thinking.* New York: Harper and Row.

Hempel, C. G. (1965). *Aspects of scientific explanation.* New York: Macmillan.

Hempel, C. G. (1966). *Philosophy of natural science.* Englewood Cliff, NJ: Prentice-Hall.

Ho, D. Y. F. (1988). Asian psychology: A dialogue on indigenization and beyond. In A. C. Paranjpe, D. Y. F. Ho, & R. W. Rieber (Eds.), *Asian contributions to psychology* (pp. 53–77). New York: Praeger.

Ho, D. (1993). Relational orientation in Asian social psychology. In U. Kim & J. W. Berry (Eds.), *Indigenous psychologies: Research and experience in cultural context.* Newbury Park: Sage.

Ho, D. Y. F. (1998). Indigenous psychologies: Asian perspectives. *Journal of Cross-Cultural Psychology, 29,* 88–103.

Hofstede, G. (2001). *Culture's consequences: International differences in work related values.* Thousand Oaks, CA: Sage Publications.

Hong, Y. (2009). A dynamic constructivist approach to culture: Moving from describing culture to explaining culture. In R. S. Wyer, C.-Y. Chiu,

& Y. –Y. Hong (Eds.), *Understanding culture: Theory, research and application* (pp. 3–23). New York: Psychology Press.

Husserl, E. (1970). *The crisis of European sciences and transcendental phenomenology: An introduction to phenomenological philosophy.* Trans. by E. Hysserl. Evanston: Northwestern University Press.

Hwang, K. K. (1987). Face and Favor: The Chinese power game. *American Journal of Sociology, 92,* 944–974.

Hwang, K. K. (1988). *Confucianism and East Asian modernization* (in Chinese). Taipei: Chu-Liu Book Co.

Hwang, K. K. (1995). *Knowledge and action: A social-psychological interpretation of Chinese cultural tradition* (In Chinese). Taipei: Sin-Li.

Hwang, K. K. (2000). The discontinuity hypothesis of modernity and constructive realism: The philosophical basis of indigenous psychology. *Hong Kong Journal of Social Sciences, 18,* 1–32.

Hwang, K. K. (2001). *The logic of social sciences* (in Chinese). Taipei, Taiwan: Psychological Publishing.

Hwang, K. K. (2003a). *The logic of social sciences* (2nd ed.; in Chinese). Taipei, Taiwan: Psychological Publishing.

Hwang, K. K. (2003b). Critique of the methodology of empirical research on individual modernity in Taiwan. *Asian Journal of Social Psychology, 6,* 241–262.

Hwang, K. K. (2003c). In search of a new paradigm for cultural psychology. *Asian Journal of Social Psychology, 6,* 287–291.

Hwang, K. K. (2005). From anticolonialism to postcolonialism: The emergence of Chinese indigenous psychology in Taiwan. *International Journal of Psychology, 40*(4): 228–238.

Hwang, K. K. (2006). Constructive realism and Confucian relationalism: An epistemological strategy for the development of indigenous psychology. In U. Kim, K. S. Yang, & K. K. Hwang (Eds.), *Indigenous and cultural psychology: understanding people in context* (pp. 73–108). New York: Springer.

Hwang, K. K. (2009). *Confucian relationalism: Philosophical reflection, theoretical construction and empirical research* (in Chinese). Taipei, Taiwan: Psychological Publishing.

Hwang, K. K. (2011a). The Mandala model of self. *Psychological Studies, 56*(4): 329–334.

Hwang, K. K. (2011b). *A proposal for scientific revolution in psychology* (in Chinese). Taipei: Psychological Publishing.

Hwang, K. K. (2011c). Reification of culture in indigenous psychologies: Merit or mistake? *Social Epistemology, 25*(2): 125–131.

Hwang, K. K. (2012). *Foundations of Chinese psychology: Confucian social relations*. New York: Springer.

Hwang, K. K. (2013). The construction of culture-inclusive theories by multiple philosophical paradigms. *Social Epistemology Review and Reply Collective, 2* (7): 46–58.

Hwang, K. K. (2015). Cultural system vs. pan-cultural dimensions: Philosophical reflection on approaches for indigenous psychology. *Journal for the Theory of Social Behaviour, 45* (1): 1–24.

Hwang, K. K (2016). Philosophical switch for the third wave of psychology in the age of globalization. In A. Tsuda & K. K. Hwang (Eds). *Japanese Psychological Research. Special Issue: The Construction of Culture-Inclusive Approaches in Psychology.* 58(2): 97–109.

Hwang, K. K. (2017a). Confucian ethical healing and psychology of self-cultivation. *Research in the Social Scientific Study of Religion, 28,* 60.

Hwang, K. K. (2017b). *Dialects for the subjectivity of Confucian cultural system.* Taipei: Wunan Book.

Hwang, K. K. (2017c). Intellectual intuition and Kant's epistemology. *Asian Journal of Social Psychology, 20*(2): 150–154.

Hwang, K. K. (2018a). *Logic of social sciences* (4th ed.) (in Chinese). Taipei, Taiwan: Psychological Publishing.

Hwang, K. K. (2018b). *Inner sageliness and outer kingliness: The accomplishment and unfolding of Confucianism.* Taipei, Taiwan: Psychological Publishing.

Hwang, K. K., & Yang, C. F. (2000) (Eds.). *Asian Journal of Social Psychology,* 3(3): 183–297.

Hwang, K. K., & Yang, K. S. (1972). Studies on individual modernity and social orientation. *Bulletin of the Institute of Ethnology, Academia Sinica, 32,* 245–278.

Hwang, K. K., Shiah, Y. J., & Yit, K. T. (2017). Eastern philosophies and psychology: Towards psychology of self-cultivation. *Frontiers in psychology, 8,* 1083.

Jaffe, A. (1964). Symbolism in the visual arts. In C. G. Jung, (Ed.), *Man and His Symbols.* New York: Dell Publishing.

Jahoda, G. (2016). On the rise and decline of 'indigenous psychology'. *Culture & Psychology, 22*(2): 169–181.

Jaspers, K. (1953). *The origin and goal of history.* London: Routledge & Kegan Paul.

Jullien, F.(1998). *Un sage est sans idée ou l'autre de la philosophie.* Paris: Seuil.

Jung, C.G. (1964). *Man and his symbols.* New York : Anchor Press.

Kant, I. (1781/1965). *Critique of pure reason*. Trans. by N. K. Smith. New York: St Martin's Press.

Kim, U. (2000). Indigenous, cultural, and cross-cultural psychology: A theoretical, conceptual, and epistemological analysis. *Asian Journal of Social Psychology, 3*(3): 265–287.

Kim, U. (2001). Culture, science, and indigenous psychologies. In D. Matsumoto (Ed.), *The handbook of culture and psychology* (pp. 51–76). Oxford: Oxford University Press.

Kim, U. E., & Berry, J. W. (1993). *Indigenous psychologies: Research and experience in cultural context*. Thousand Oaks, CA: Sage Publications.

Kim, U., & Park, Y. S. (2006). The scientific foundation of indigenous and cultural psychology. In *Indigenous and Cultural Psychology* (pp. 27–48), Boston, MA: Springer.

Kim, U., Park, Y. S., & Park, D. (2000). The challenge of cross-cultural psychology: The role of the indigenous psychologies. *Journal of Cross-Cultural Psychology, 31*, 63–75.

Kim, U., Yang, K. S., & Hwang, K. K. (2006). Contributions to indigenous and cultural psychology. In *Indigenous and Cultural Psychology* (pp. 3–25). Springer, Boston, MA.

Kramer, D. A. (1990). Conceptualizing wisdom: The primacy of affect-cognition relations. In R. J. Sternberg (Ed.), *Wisdom: Its nature, origins, and development* (pp. 279–323). New York: Cambridge University Press.

Kramer, D. A. (2000). Wisdom as a classical source of human strength: Conceptualization and empirical inquiry. *Journal of Social and Clinical Psychology, 19*, 83–101.

Kuhn, T. (1987). What are scientific revolutions? In L. Krüger, L. J. Datson, and M. Heidelberger (Eds.), *The probabilistic revolution* (pp. 7–22). Cambridge, MA: MIT Press.

Kwok, D. W. Y. (1965/1987). *Scientism in Chinese thought, 1900–1950*. New Haven, CN: Yale University Press.

Lakatos, I. (1970). Falsification and the methodology of scientific research programmes. In I. Lakatos & A. Musgrave (Eds.), *Criticism and the growth of knowledge*. Cambridge: Cambridge University Press.

Lakatos, I. (1971). History of science and its rational reconstructions. In *PSA 1970* (pp. 91–136). Springer, Dordrecht.

Laudan, L. (1977). *Progress and its problems: Toward a theory of scientific growth*. London: Routledge & Kegan Paul.

Lee, Y. T. (2011). Book review (Review of the book *The Oxford Handbook of Chinese Psychology*). *International Journal of Cross Cultural Management, 11*(2): 269–272.

Leong, F. T., & Blustein, D. L. (2000). Toward a global vision of counseling psychology. *The Counseling Psychologist, 28*(1): 5–9.

Leventhal, G. S. (1976). The distribution of reward and resources in groups and organizations. In L. Berkowitz (Ed.), *Advances in experimental social psychology* (Vol. 9) (pp. 91–131). New York: Academic Press.

Leventhal, G. S. (1980). What should be done with equality theory? In K. J. Gergen, M. S. Greenberg, & R. H. Willis (Eds.), *Social exchange: Advance in theory and research* (pp. 27–55). New York: Plenum Press.

Lévi-Strauss, C. (1976). *Tristes Tropiques*. London: Penguin.

Levy-Bruhl, L. (1910/1966). *How natives think*. Trans. by L. A. Clare. New York: Washington Square Press.

Lin, Y. S. (1979). *The crisis of Chinese consciousness: Radical anti-traditionalism in the May fourth era*. Madison: The University of Wisconsin Press.

Marsella, A. J. (1998). Toward a global community psychology: Meeting the needs of changing world. *American Psychologist 53* (12): 1282–1291.

Morris, M. W., Chiu, C. Y., & Liu, Z. (2015). Polycultural psychology. *Annual Review of Psychology, 66*, 631–659.

Needham, J. (1969). *Grand titration: Science and society in east and west*. Toronto: University of Toronto Press.

Needham, J. (1978). *Clerks and craftsman: China and the west: Lectures and addresses on the history of science and technology*. Cambridge: Cambridge University Press.

Piaget, J. (1972). *The Principle of genetic epistemology*. Trans. by W. Mays. London: Knowledge & Kegan Paul.

Poortinga, Y. H. (1996). Indigenous psychology: Scientific ethnocentrism in a new guise? In J. Pandey, D. Sinha & D. P. S. Bhawuk (Eds.), *Asian contributions to cross-cultural psychology* (pp. 59–71). Thousand Oaks, CA: Sage.

Poortinga, Y. H. (1999). Do differences in behavior imply a need for different psychologies? *Applied Psychology: An International Review, 48*(4): 419–432.

Popper. K. (1963). *Conjectures and refutations: The growth of scientific knowledge*. London: Routledge & Kegan Paul.

Popper, K. (1972). *Objective knowledge: An evolutionary approach*. Oxford: Oxford University Press.

Rawls, J. (1971). *A theory of justice*. Cambridge, MA: Belknap Press of Harvard University Press.

Schlick, M. (1936). Meaning and verification. *The Philosophical Review, 45*, 339–369.

Shen, V. (1994). *Confucianism, Taoism and constructive realism*. Bruck: WUV-Universitäsverlag.

Shweder, R. A. (1990). Cultural psychology: What is it? In J.W. Stigler, R. A. Shweder, & G. Herdt (Eds.), *Cultural psychology: Essays on comparative human development* (pp. 1–4). Cambridge: Cambridge University Press.

Shweder, R. A. (1996). The "mind" of cultural psychology. In P. Baltes and U. Staudinger (Eds.), *Interactive minds: Life-span perspectives on the social foundations of cognition* (pp. 430–436). New York: Cambridge University Press.

Shweder, R. A. (2000). The psychology of practice and the practice of the three psychologies. *Asian Journal of Social Psychology, 3*, 207–222

Shweder, R. A., Goodnow, J., Hatano, G., LeVine, R. A., Markus, H., & Miller, P. (1998). The cultural psychology of development: One mind, many mentalities. In W. Damon & R. M. Lerner (Eds.), *Handbook of child psychology: Theoretical models of human development* (pp. 865–937). Hoboken, NJ: John Wiley & Sons Inc.

Sinha, D. (1984). Psychology in the context of third world development. *International Journal of Psychology, 19*, 17–29.

Sinha, D. (1986). *Psychology in a third world country: The Indian experience*. New Delhi: Sage.

Sternberg, R. J. (2000). Intelligence and wisdom. In R. J. Sternberg (Ed.), *Handbook of Intelligence* (pp. 629–647). New York: Cambridge University Press.

Stotland, E., & Canon, L. K. (1972). *Social psychology: A cognitive approach*. Philadelphia: Saunders Limited.

Sundararajan, L. (2015). Indigenous psychology: Grounding science in culture, why and how? *Journal for the Theory of Social Behaviour, 45*(1): 64–81.

Sundararajan, L., Misra, G., & Marsella, A. J. (2013). Indigenous approaches to assessment, diagnosis, and treatment of mental disorders. In F. A. Paniagua & A.-M. Yamada (Eds.), *Handbook of multicultural mental health* (pp. 69–88). Oxford: Academic Press.

Sundararajan, L., Kim, U., & Park, Y.-S. (2017). Indigenous psychologies. In J. Stein (Ed.), *Reference module in neuroscience and biobehavioral psychology* (pp. 1–7). Amsterdam: Elsevier.

Taylor, C. (1989). *Sources of the self: The making of the modern identity*. Cambridge, MA: Harvard University Press.

Taylor, C. (1992). Modernity and the rise of the public sphere. The Tanner Lectures on Human Values, Stanford University. Vol. 14, pp. 203–260.

Triandis, H. C. (1996). The psychological measurement of cultural syndromes. *American Psychologist, 51*, 407–415.

Triandis, H. C. (2000). Dialectics between cultural and cross-cultural psychology. *Asian Journal of Social Psychology, 3*, 185–195.

Tu, W. M. (1998). Probing the three bonds and five relationships in Confucian humanism. In G. A. De Vos (Ed.), *Confucianism and the family* (pp. 121–136). Albany: State University of New York Press.

Tylor, E. B. (1871). *Primitive culture: Researches into the development of mythology, philosophy, religion, art, and custom* (Vol. 2). London: John Murray.

Vaisey, S. (2010). What people want: Rethinking poverty, culture, and educational attainment. *Annals of the American Academy of Political and Social Science, 629*, 75–101.

Wallner, F. (1994). *Constructive realism: Aspects of a new epistemological movement*. Wien: W. Braumuller.

Wallner, F. G., & Jandl, M. J. (2006). The importance of constructive realism for the indigenous psychologies approach. In U. Kim, K. S. Yang, & K. K. Hwang (Eds.), *Indigenous and cultural psychology* (pp. 49–72). Boston, MA: Springer.

Walsh, B. J., & Middleton, J. R. (1984). *The transforming vision: Shaping a Christian world view*. Downers Grove, IL: Inter-Varsity Press.

Weber, E. U., & Morris, M. W. (2010). Culture and judgment and decision making: The constructivist turn. *Perspectives on Psychological Science, 5*(4): 410–419.

Weber, M. (1921/1963). *The sociology of religion*. Boston: Beacon Press.

Weber, M. (1930/1992). *The protestant ethic and the spirit of capitalism*. Trans. by T. Parsons. London: Routledge.

Wittgenstein, L. (1922). *Tractatus logico-philosophicus*, with an introduction by B. Russell; trans. by D. F. Pears and B. F. McGuinnies. London: Routledge & Kegan Raul.

Wittgenstein, L. (1945/1958). *Philosophical investigation*. Ed. & trans. by G. E. M. Anscombe. New York: Macmillan.

Yang, K. S. (1993). Why do we need to develop an indigenous Chinese psychology? *Indigenous Psychological Research in Chinese Societies, 1*, 6–88. (In Chinese).

Yang, K.S. (1997). Indigenizing westernized Chinese psychology. In M. H. Bond (Ed.), *Working at the interface of cultures: Eighteen lives in social science* (pp. 62–76). London: Routledge.

Yang, K. S. (2003). Methodological and theoretical issues on psychological traditionality and modernity research in an Asian society: In response to Kwang-Kuo Hwang and beyond. *Asian Journal Social Psychology, 6*, 287–288.

Yang, K. S. (2012). Indigenous psychology, westernized psychology, and indigenized psychology: A non-western psychologist. *Chang Gung Journal of Humanities and Social Sciences*, 5(1): 1–32.

Yang, K. S. & Wen, C.I. (1982). *The sinicization of research in social and behavioral science.* Taipei: Academia sinica: Institute of Ethnology.

Cambridge Elements ☰

Psychology and Culture

Kenneth D. Keith

University of San Diego

Kenneth D. Keith is author or editor of more than 160 publications on cross-cultural psychology, quality of life, intellectual disability, and the teaching of psychology. He was the 2017 president of the Society for the Teaching of Psychology.

About the Series

Elements in Psychology and Culture features authoritative surveys and updates on key topics in cultural, cross-cultural, and indigenous psychology. Authors are internationally recognized scholars whose work is at the forefront of their subdisciplines within the realm of psychology and culture.

Cambridge Elements≡

Psychology and Culture

Elements in the Series

The Continuing Growth of Cross-Cultural Psychology: A First-Person Annotated Chronology
Walter J. Lonner

Measuring and Interpreting Subjective Wellbeing in Different Cultural Contexts: A Review and Way Forward
Robert A. Cummins

The Nature and Challenges of Indigenous Psychologies
Carl Martin Allwood

Global Changes in Children's Lives
Uwe P. Gielen and Sunghun Kim

Gene–Culture Interactions: Toward an Explanatory Framework
Joni Y. Sasaki and Heewon Kwon

Culture-Inclusive Theories: An Epistemological Strategy
Kwang-Kuo Hwang

Acculturation: A Personal Journey across Cultures
John W. Berry

A full series listing is available at: www.cambridge.org/EPAC

Printed in the United States
By Bookmasters